PRICKLE IN A DREAM
A tale of an African orphan

PRICKLE IN A DREAM
A tale of an African orphan

PAUL MASEMBE

A Division of adoptamum.com

Copyright © 2012 Paul Masembe.

All rights reserved. No part of this book may be used or reproduced by any means, graphic, electronic, or mechanical, including photocopying, recording, taping or by any information storage retrieval system without the written permission of the publisher except in the case of brief quotations embodied in critical articles and reviews.

This is a work of fiction. All of the characters, names, incidents, organizations and dialogue in this novel are either the products of the author's imagination or are used fictitiously.

Inner Light Publishing books may be ordered through booksellers or by contacting:

Inner Light Publishing
A Division of Adoptamum.com
www.adoptamum.com
innerlightpublishing@gmail.com

Because of the dynamic nature of the Internet, any web addresses or links contained in this book may have changed since publication and may no longer be valid. The views expressed in this work are solely those of the author and do not necessarily reflect the views of the publisher and the publisher hereby disclaims any responsibility for them.

The author of this book does not dispense medical advice or prescribe the use of any technique as a form of treatment for physical, emotional, or medical problems without the advice of a physician, either directly or indirectly. The intent of the author is only to offer information of a general nature to help you in your quest for emotional and spiritual well-being. In the event you use any of the information in this book for yourself, which is your constitutional right, the author and the publisher assume no responsibility for your actions.

ISBN: **978-0-9872818-4-5** (sc)
ISBN: **978-0-9872818-5-2** (e)

Printed in Australia

Acknowledgements

For my family and my friends.
Thank you for encouraging me to put this book together.
I could barely glimpse a love like you have shown.

Thank you, my dear Heart, for this life and love we are sharing

Contents

Chapter One	My Childhood	1
Chapter Two	Journey to Manhood	23
Chapter Three	The rainy season	36
Chapter Four	The Hush Times	46
Chapter Five	The Great Trek to Independence	71
Chapter Six	2012 Update	96

Introduction

Masembe, fondly referred to as Mase by his mother, was brought up in a simple and humble household characterized by poverty, diseases and all sorts of ailments. Through extreme work and pain, his mother managed to send him to school as his father cared less about his education and welfare. In short, his mother was the bread winner. Unfortunately, she became very ill and unable to financially support the family. Being the first born, Mase was expected to be the caretaker of the family. He goes through a lot of adversities and difficulties and as time went on, even his own family became a pain in the neck. Fortunately, he got a philanthropist who helped him with some of the responsibilities. Here he comes out with determination to use his gift to highlight what an orphaned child goes through. This book is going to be used as a potential source of hope for the less privileged in the less developed world.

Paul Masembe

Chapter 1

My Childhood

"If you cannot go to the farm and work like other women of your age, then do not bother asking me for school fees," my father bellowed furiously.

I was outside our small grass thatched house with my ear to the wall and I could hear every word that my father said to mother when she asked for my school fees. It was not my intention to eavesdrop but after mother had assured me that she was going to convince father about my education, I was so eager to know what they were to discuss. At only five, I could not understand why father always treated mother cruelly. I might have been a child, but I could sense that all was not well with my family. On hearing what my father had to say, I ran as far as my legs could carry me. I only made a stop under a mango tree in the back yard. Out of the blue, tears profusely streaked down my gaunt cheeks.

I grew to hate my father so much and admired families where the father could sit down with his wife and children and tell one another stories. I wondered how a father could laugh with his children and wife and only wished I belonged to such family. I could see children in the neighbourhood playing hide and seek, board games like "omweso" and football with their fathers. I envied such children because they seemed to be on good terms with their parents. They discussed family matters freely with one another and managed to send their children to school though they did not have much. While we felt comfortable in our clothes that we wore until they could outsize us, such fathers always bought new clothes for their children every Christmas. They ate bread for breakfast and meat was rarely missing on their Sunday menu.

As I was still thinking through all this, I heard a soft voice which was sweet as fresh banana juice calling out, "Mase . . . Mase . . . Masembe".

It was my mother searching for me. I never wanted her to know that I had heard what father had said to her. I wiped my tears, cleared my voice and then replied in a broken tone, "Yes mother, I am coming." Then I ran steadily towards the house.

On arrival, my Mother handed me roasted maize. She then noticed something in my eyes and asked, "Masembe, why are your eyes red? Have you been crying? What has happened to you?"

"I . . . I was playing with my friends in the neighbourhood, and Peter accidentally pricked my eye," I replied.

"Okay, finish up that maize as I also finish peeling this cassava for supper."

This is how life has been in the whole of my life. My childhood memories are very few, dark and coupled with pain and misery. At the age of ten, I had never stepped into a classroom; nor had any of my siblings. My mother never had money and my father would always claim that he earned only very little, which could not be enough to finance our education.

In our ancestral home, Bukabi village, Kakooge sub country, Nakasogola District in Uganda, lies a place where the prickle in the dream started. I was born in the year 1982, at a time when this village was wallowing in dire poverty, acute water shortage, high levels of illiteracy, a good number of vulnerable children, many orphans, high school dropout rates and diseases such as HIV/AIDS. The population depended mostly on subsistence farming.

More or less like the general population, we stayed in a single-roomed grass thatched house, just big enough to accommodate the seven of us. We had a small garden and we used to grow food just for home use. We mostly planted cassava, sweet potatoes, maize and beans.

My mother was a very hardworking, caring and loving woman. The fact that she was brought up in a very poor but humble family gave her no chance to be educated. She used to stay at home and work in the garden.

My father was an alcoholic, very serious, scary, aggressive, argumentative, rude, thoughtless, irritating and authoritarian. I never lived to enjoy the love of my father. He was a man who never played, joked or had time for his family. There was nothing like intimacy between us and our father. We grew up with no father's direction at all. For as long as I can remember, I was always afraid of my dad and never at any one point did I experience his love and affection. The only thing I can remember about him is the fact that he was a banker who spent most of what he earned on alcohol. He always spent most of his time away from home. This was joy for me and my siblings since we would never get to hear his scary voice at least for those few hours or days. On the other hand, my mother would always be miserable during this time, wondering where he could be. She would move from one "drinking" area to another in search of him, but usually it was in vain. After several hours or even days he would surface. He would be so dirty that if he wasn't someone I knew so well, I could easily mistake him for a mad man. The fact that he was much older compared to my mother gave him sufficient reason not to listen to her correction.

While other parents empathetically confronted ordeals, and shared secrets and findings, supporting each other where children were concerned, it wasn't the case with my mother and father. My father was irresponsible and wasn't committed at all. He would often beat her up whenever she tried to advise him on anything concerned with alcohol.

My mother would gather us up in the evenings at the fire place and would start telling us stories and sing sweet songs. She would also teach us how to count numbers 1 to 100 in Luganda and the alphabet since that was all she could do for us at that time.

One blessed, night as my parents lay in bed, my mother sweet-talked my father until he accepted to take me to school. He claimed that my siblings were still too young and that he could afford school fees for only one child. My mother decided that I should be the one to go to school since I was the eldest.

As I lay on the sacks (which was my bed) and covered myself with an old backcloth which acted as my blanket, I had a dream. In this dream my siblings and I had grown up into responsible citizens. We were at home one day and a stranger appeared. We welcomed him home and we requested him to enter into the house but he refused, saying that he was in a hurry and had limited time. As he pulled out his business card from his pocket, he said, "My name is Mayanja from Uganda Air Services Limited. I am looking for Mr. Masembe."

This befuddled my Mother and she anxiously asked, "What, has your father done wrong this time?"

"Which of you is called Mr. Masembe?" the man asked.

"I am the one," I confidently replied.

The man then said that the Organization he is working for was looking for a competent individual to train and work with their company. He further said that Mr. Masembe had been short-listed for the interviews.

At that moment, I lost a few heart beats. I was so surprised. I realized that God never forgets his people. I then remembered all the times that I could hear the sound of a plane flying in the sky, and I could just tell my siblings that one day, I would be the one above in the skies flying the plane. I asked myself so many questions to which I could not get answers. I felt like a millionaire experiencing Heaven on earth.

As the stranger and I were on our way to the company headquarters, I had my mother calling out, "Mase . . ., wake up. You are going to school today." When I woke up, I was perplexed to observe that the environment around me contrasted sharply with the grandeur of the dream. I looked on my right and my left and I could only see the same sacks and the same old backcloth.

I asked my mother," Where is Mr.Mayanja?" She failed to figure out what I was asking her, so she just moved on. At that moment, I realized that it was a dream. I always wanted to become a pilot and now the opportunity was there but only in a dream."

At that moment, my mother called out again," Mase, your tea is ready. Hurry up and we go." I went to the kitchen and I asked her, "Mom, where are we going?" She then answered, "You are starting school today. Go and shower, then take your tea and we go." My heart skipped a bit as a rush of excitement ran through my nerves. I asked her "mom, where did you get the money from?"

She told me that she had won the race of convincing my father about my education. At that moment I felt as if an angel had visited me. I felt God had come from Heaven to our house. I wondered, "My father paying my school fees? . . . pigs may fly!"

I could not fathom the joy I felt at what mother had just told me. This was what I had always wanted in my life. I could not believe that I was going to be like other children who used to wake up in the morning to go

Prickle in a Dream

to school, to do homework. What excited me most was that I was also going to start speaking the white man's language. I knew this was the turning point in my life as instead of waking up to rush for my hoe, I was going to replace it with books and pens.

I quickly bathed and wondered what I was going to wear. I then remembered my multi-coloured coat that I had kept for so long. It was the only thing left of my grandfather's souvenir. He gave it to me as a memento 6 years before he went to meet his creator. He said that it was a sign of how much he loved me and he urged me to keep it safely. I then quickly ferreted through my old box for the belt that had been my grandfather's. It had been mistakenly carried along with my property as I left his last funeral rites. I realized that it had been feasted on by the many rats that we had at home. Nevertheless, I had no choice. I forged a way of fixing it because I wanted to look smart on my first day of school. I then remembered that the only three shorts I owned were all torn and muggy. I then ran to mother and inquired what I was supposed to put on. She grinned as she remembered the only shorts she had kept for me for attending important functions. She then hurriedly went and checked in her box until she found it and presented it to me. I felt I was going to be the smartest in the whole school. I walked with my head held high and with a lot of confidence.

As my mother and I left home, I asked her "what about Wanyana, Mpagi, Seguya and Nansubuga?"

"Masembe!" she replied, "your sister Wanyana, and brother Mpagi will be due for school but still we cannot afford their school fees. Seguya is physically handicapped and will require a lot of money for his education. The only school for the physically handicapped is so expensive for us to afford.

As we moved, we passed forests and crossed a stream that border our village and another. The road was too dusty and birds chirruped in the atmosphere. I saw children of my age carrying hoes and some of them were carrying their siblings on their backs. Then I regarded myself as one of the luckiest children that were able to go to school in the village. The school was 5 km away from home. Though it was a long distance, all that mattered was getting to school as soon as possible.

As we were about to reach the school, my mother contentedly pointed to a fenceless terrain as she increased the speed at which we were moving and shouted, "Look!" she shouted, we have reached the school!"

I impulsively ran past her as I fought hard to see the school she was trying to show me. I looked at where she was pointing and all I could see was a big field with patched grass and big trees around. I could see several groups of small children gathered together under trees. As I was still wondering, my mother emphasized, "That is the school . . . your school. Hurry and we go."

As we finally reached the school, I realized that most of the pupils were dressed in very old torn clothes of different sizes and colours. I looked at myself and that was when I realized that the coat was too big for me, that my green belt was halfway broken and that my brown shorts had already lost its texture. I lost the confidence about the way I was dressed.

There were around ten children in the whole school who dressed in pink and white squared short-sleeved shirts with khaki shorts. At that moment I thought they were children who came from the same family, and that their parents bought them the same clothes. Little did I know that it was the school uniform. It was only those ten pupils who could afford to buy it. I soon realized that the school never had proper buildings.

My mother and I were later directed into the Headmaster's office. I saw a very old man who had looked like my father – an alcoholic. He had only one stool in the office and it served as his desk. He was seated on a very old, unbalanced chair and there were so many empty boxes in his office. As he saw us entering into his office, he happily rose up and welcomed us in. He greeted my mother and later me, and then asked for my name. I answered that my name is Masembe.

"So Masembe's mother," he inquired, "what can I do for you?"

My mother replied, "I want Masembe to start studying from here. So what is expected of us?"

He replied, "So which school and class has he been in?"

My mother replied, "Well, he has not been studying, but he is a bright and very hardworking boy."

"So does that mean he should start from nursery?" he asked.

"No," my mother replied. "You understand the situation in this village. We do not have the money for nursery, so please allow him to start from primary three, and in addition, he is too old for nursery; he is already seven years old."

My mother pleaded with him, until they came to a consensus that I should start from primary two. It was all smiles for me and my mother. The fact that I was going to step into a class was a feather in the cap for my mother.

"You are required," the headmaster said, "to pay two hundred shillings for the application form, eight thousand shillings for his school fees, and three thousand shillings for a uniform, shoes, books and pencils. Do you have the money now so that he can start his classes?"

"No sir!" She replied.

He then told my mother to go back home as I would stay and study. He took me to the class to start my first day. I was so happy that for the first time I was entering into a class room. To my disappointment, he led me to a place under a tree and he told me that I should sit down and start studying like other pupils. I found around twenty pupils sitting on the wooden benches and they were making a lot of noise. They were all fighting for the only three small benches which were not enough for all of them. I saw that 99% of the children in the class did not differ so much from me. We all walked barefoot and most of us were malnourished. I looked at all of them carefully. They all looked younger than I was. I started wondering if I was in the right class. As I was still struggling to look for where to sit, an old man, who I later realized was the teacher, appeared. All of a sudden, the whole class went silent as they settled down.

"Do we have any new comers?" asked the teacher. Then he looked around and recognized that I was the only new pupil. Everyone set their eyes on me. I shyly stood up, looked around and finally looked down on the ground.

"What is your name?" the teacher asked.

As I prepared to answer, I coughed so loudly that all the pupils laughed.

"He has broken the cup," one pupil murmured.

"Yes, and look at his coat," the other added as the laughter grew louder and became so uncontrollable. As if it was intentional, the teacher told me to sit down without mentioning my name and he continued with what he had planned for the day. From that incident, the pupils nicknamed me "cup-breaker" because of the whopping cough that I had.

At around 12:30pm we were released to go back home. I started on the journey back home and I saw many children going my way. Most of them pulled out sugar canes from polythene bags and ate them along the way back home. Others would even run to the nearby bush and get mangoes.

I walked straight until I reached home. The next day, mother gave me two hundred shillings for the application, a 32 paged book and a pencil. From that day, I started going to school alone leaving my mother and

Wanyana working in the garden. I used to have one book for all the four subjects that were being taught at school. I never bothered about the uniform and the shoes since most of the children lacked them too.

"No, please, do not do that . . . I promise I will never do it again," I shouted feebly as Mr Ssemalulu pinched my ear so hard. The heat was so much and my ear hurt me so badly.

"He started it all . . . He came . . . and . . ." I sobbed as Mr. Ssemalulu spanked me a slap.

"You are going to be expelled!" He snapped.

I cried so loudly and regretted why I had picked a fight with that boy in my class. It was obvious that he started it, but no one seemed to believe me. He had pushed my head as if it were a duck. With all the smartness I had left home with that morning, I could not just let him disorganise my hair just for a cup of porridge. My heel of Achilles was fighting, and I could not hold back when this short, undersized cruel, filthy lad abused me. This was the most obstinate, mulish and defiant pupil in the whole school. Of course he was in the same class with me and I was older than him, but where could I find a reason to really let him step on my feet?

From the day I reported to school, I heard the pupils calling him "Mulwanyi". I always believed that it was his name and not until that day did I find out that it was just a nickname to mean warrior. Everyone in class feared him, not because he was too powerful, but because he was too brutal. He usually bullied new comers and

Prickle in a Dream

took advantage of them. I had been in this school for a month, and he had never found a reason to torment me.

"This jerk found me reading and he abused and slapped me." Mulwanyi snarled as he walked, turning around pompously. He made a forward step and continued, "Imagine, I was trying to do this mathematics number that we had all failed to get an answer to. Just as I was about to get the solution to the number, this good for nothing pig came and slapped me," he convinced the teacher.

He was so lucky that he knew how to convince the teachers so well and he made me guilty. Mr Ssemalulu believed that I was the cause of bad blood and that I had to be castigated and punished severely.

"No Sir! It is not true. He is the one who . . ." But before I could even defend myself, Mr, Semalulu shouted, "shut up!!"

"He even said that I come from a very poor family, just because he looked at my once white shirt which had turned brown," Mulwanyi continued.

All the pupils in the whole school gathered on the scene to see who had fought the "title holder". I felt so small and lost all my bravery. I could hardly utter out any more word because people kept on shouting and accusing me falsely.

"We do not want undisciplined and rowdy pupils in this school. If you came here to show your disruptive behavior, we shall not tolerate you. You must abide by all the school rules and regulations. If there is a problem, you have to report to the teacher on duty. Are your ears open, you wild pig?" he bellowed furiously. "The next time you are caught in such a mess, you will face the disciplinary committee's intense punishment or, even worse, you may be dismissed," barked the angry teacher as he released my almost smoldering ear.

I felt so embarrassed. The words of the teacher rang in my ears and I wondered what could happen if my mother, who knew me as the most disciplined boy in the whole village, heard what the teacher had just told me. God forbid, she would be very miserable, depressed and disappointed in me for the bad demeanor. I felt so saddened and I just sat alone in the shadow of the tree as all the other pupils parted ways talking about the incident.

As I thought about all this with my eyes red and tearing, someone touched my shoulder. I frightfully turned to find out who it was. He was a nice-looking, tall, brown-skinned boy. He looked at me with a lot of sympathy and I felt reassured. I looked at him critically and he was different from the rest of the pupils. He differed very much from most of the pupils in the whole school. He had a healthy skin and he was very smart in his school uniform. His hair was well kempt and he was wearing shoes unlike most of the pupils. It seemed to me that he was from a well to do family.

"My name is Mukasa and I am in primary four. I saw what had happened earlier on with Mulwanyi and I know that it was not at all your fault. I am so sorry about what you had to go through. Anyway he is a very stubborn and cruel boy and everyone knows him for that," said the boy in a calm and comforting tone.

"Everyone here fears him because of his boorish character. He is ill-mannered, especially to new comers in the school. To avoid embarrassment, people only have to pretend being on his side, because if one tries to criticize him, one becomes the next victim. Please stop crying and wipe those tears away. You are not alone. I feel your pain," Mukasa added.

"He just found me sitting on the bench while taking porridge that my mother had packed for me as I left home in the morning. He asked me where I had got it from since the school does not provide lunch and porridge at break time. I told him that I had come with it from home. He asked me to hand over the cup to him, but I told him that I was very hungry so that I could not give him my porridge. He started beating me and pushing my head. He told me that I brought the porridge just to show off. I got hot under the collar and hit him on his back as well." I recounted the day's events.

"He is a very naughty and impish boy. He does not respect anyone, not even the teachers. He thinks he has the authority to do anything he wishes. At one time he also slapped and abused me because I refused to give him my pen. He also told me that I put on shoes to show that I come from a very wealthy family, but all I could do was to ignore him since I could not fight him," Mukasa said.

"Why have the teachers not yet dismissed him from school?" I asked.

He gave a mocking smile and said, "he is a son of the Local Council Chairman. His uncle is also on the board of governors committee. It is therefore very difficult for the administrator to expel him from school as he pays his fees in time. He usually uses his father's and uncle's title to hit his rivals below the belt. He oppresses children from poor families and nobody reprimands him. He is really getting too big for his boots. Besides, he is a very cunning boy who knows how to convince anyone that he is not in the wrong."

He held my right hand up as he slowly pulled me to stand up, "I know things are going to be fine. Let us now go back to class and I want to see you before you go back home."

That day our class was released before theirs. I sat down and waited for him as all the pupils in my class found their way back to their homes. After around 30 minutes he appeared with all smiles on his face.

"I thought you had already left," he shouted from a distance. "I saw the pupils in your class leaving before our science teacher concluded our lesson. He was trying to give us homework to do during the weekend. Can you imagine he has given us 50 numbers and he wants them done by Monday? Anyway how are you this evening?" he said as he finally reached where I was.

"I am fine, and you?" I asked.

"Well, I am fine too. I wanted to take you to my home and so you visit me. Is it okay with you?" he asked as he stared at me right in the eye.

"Isn't your home too far?" I asked him. "No! Not at all. Are you seeing the other junction just after the hut?" He asked as he pointed at a junction a few meters away from the school compound, "that is where I branch from, and then I make a few more steps until I reach home. Let's go and see."

We moved until we reached his home. They had a very good compound with flowers everywhere with a barbed wire fence. I still remember its fine greenery and the cozy environment around their home. Their house was brick-constructed and ventilated with fashionable ventilators, aluminum windows and doors. They had a kraal which contained four big cows, a sty with 2 pigs which were busy grunting and a very big banana plantation. I started wondering how rich Mukasa's family was. I really wanted to set my eyes on the "man" in that family. All my senses were still being carried away by the sight of everything when he called out, "Masembe!!" I never heard him until he called out the 3rd time. "Masembe, please enter. This is where I live," he said.

I felt embarrassed to cross the threshold with my dusty, dirty bare feet. Their house looked so tidy, but after a few minutes, I heard his mother's soft voice telling me to enter. We entered into the house. His mother, who was sitting down on a green mat trying to weave her basket, welcomed me warmly. She stood up to hug her son and finally me. I still feel the warm embrace I received from her. Mukasa hurriedly took his bag to his bedroom and changed his outfit. His mother wore her spectacles and looked like one of the educated women around.

She told me to sit in the soft sofas. I felt like a king as I quickly settled my back in the sofas. I noticed that there was a big framed picture of some man hanging in the middle of the sitting room but it was marked with a sign of the cross. I peeped into the next room and saw a girl busy preparing an aroma-packed dish which made my intestines to rumble. After a few minutes, Mukasa came back with a glass of juice and handed it over to me. I took it hurriedly for it really tasted so good. His mother then stood up to go and check if the food was ready.

I asked Mukasa where his father was and he pointed at the big framed picture as he said, "My father died a year ago due to high blood pressure. He was a very loving and kind man. I really loved daddy. He used to accompany me to school every day and he never refused to help me with my homework. I used to study in a good international school, but after daddy's death, mummy could not afford taking me to that school in the morning and fetching me in the evening, so we had to look for a nearby school and besides, the school fees there was quite a lot. May his soul rest in eternal peace," he said sorrowfully. I empathetically realized the lingering sense of the loss of his father.

After a few minutes, we were called to the dining room. One could easily realize the mixture of eagerness and apprehension written on my face. We entered into the dining room and sat down. The food looked so appetizing and so spicy. After his mother led us in the prayers, we started eating. I hastily masticated the pieces of meat that were placed on my place before I could even taste the Matooke. The way the meat and the heavy gravy tasted knocked the socks off me and I started longing for another piece on my plate. As luck may have it, Mukasa added his two pieces to my plate claiming that he was already "full". I quickly finished them too before I started on my Matooke and rice until we all finished up our food.

As I gesticulated to his mother and their maid and made a few steps out of their compound, his mother called Mukasa and they started talking in whispers. Mukasa suddenly called me back. He went into their house and came back with a very big collection of attires. I nearly jumped out of my skin when he handed it over to me. As I was trying to kneel down to thank them, his mother softly said, "No! It is okay. You do not have to kneel down. It is getting late, just stand up and go home. We have been keeping those clothes and shoes for some good time ever since they became so small that they could hardly fit Mukasa. We have actually just been looking for a person to give them to. Send our regards to your family members. Mukasa, please give him a push as he goes back home," she added.

I left their compound with my head up. I could hardly believe it. It was beyond me why they chose to give them to someone like me. I started imagining myself starting to put on shoes, expensive clothes and sweaters.

Mukasa escorted me for some short distance and later said that he had to rush back home. I hugged and thanked him endlessly. I felt I had found a real rescuer. He wished me a safe journey and promised to see me the coming Monday. Though it was getting dark, that wasn't an issue on my mind. All I wanted was to reach home so that I could show mother all those new shoes, new clothes, new shorts, ehh, new everything. "Imagine me entering class the next day with shoes on, well kept hair, a tie and very clean and "new" clothes! Everyone will start staring at me as if I were the next president of this country. My mother is really going to be caught unawares," I talked to myself as I went back home.

There were so many clothes of different sizes that everyone got something that fitted very well. My mother missed out but she was as happy as Larry when we were all trying to fit in our "new" clothes. I found that there were three pairs of shoes and two of them fitted me whereas the 3rd one fitted Mpagi. I also found a relatively old school uniform shirt. Though I never found the school shorts, I was grateful to God that I was going to put on a uniform for the first time the following Monday.

After we had shared everything amongst ourselves, my mother innocently asked, "Mase . . . where have you got all this from?"

"Mother", it is God! Today started as a bad day for me at school. This bad boy Mulwanyi fought me, and the teacher came and wanted to punish me instead. As I was there trying to think through all this, an angel appeared" I explained.

"An Angel appeared?" she asked incredulously, "You mean angels stay on earth?"

"Mother, the Angel of the day is called Mukasa. He took me to his home and his mother gave me all this. I even ate meat, matooke, rice and . . . juice. I even wished it was my home. They welcomed me so well. I never wanted to leave." I confided.

I saw the weekend was surely too long for me since I very much yearned to put on my new attire. On Monday morning, I woke up so early, even before anyone at home. I bathed so quickly and put on my best ever clothes. For the first time, I put on shoes. I knew even teachers were going to be surprised at the sight of me. I

Prickle in a Dream

walked smartly from home to school. Despite the fact that the road was too dusty, I could hardly allow any dirt to cling on my shoes. I even lost count of the number of times I cleaned my shoes before reaching school.

Finally I reached school . . . "Wow!" was the expression on everyone's face. I felt so proud and realized that even the walking style had changed. I first went to Mukasa's class and showed him how smart I was before proceeding to mine. That day was a day to remember. I paid so much attention to the teachers as they were teaching and I wanted to answer each and every question that was being asked.

Meanwhile, my father had become a rolling stone since his drinking habits had driven him away, making him incompetent at work and thus creating trouble for him with his superiors. My mother would struggle a lot to get some money from him to pay for my school fees. I do not ever remember her paying my school fees in time. I was always dismissed from school due to school fees arrears. Even when he had the money, he would first calculate how much he had to spend on his alcohol and only the balance would go to my school fees.

The time came soon when no one would offer him a job. He had also been to prison many times due to his alcoholic and abusive behavior.

I was forced out of school in my primary five since the headmaster had begun disbelieving my perpetual excuses. My mother did not have money to send me back to school and the only thing that my father thought about was alcohol. We had become a burden to him and any single coin he spent on us hurt him.

I remember him coming home one afternoon while drunk. He asked my mother for food. When my mother told him that there was no food since we had already eaten what was prepared and never expected him to return home so that she hadn't kept any for him, my father answered by saying that he was the head of the home who could come any time or day when he pleased and that he deserved some respect in his home. He then began to throw cups and plates at the walls while flipping everything that he came across.

In his drunken state, he could make one loud roar that could make us flee to different places. The yelling turned into beatings. My mother was beaten so hard that the only way she could defend herself was by running out of the house. This however did not stop my father. He pursued her, pelting beer bottles at her and yelling disgusting things. He pulled her by the hair and began to denude her for everyone to see. My mother was making a soundless cry as the neighbors cheered on. This was so embarrassing to her. As she couldn't take on the naked shame, she then dashed back into the house.

One day mother gave my father an alternative. She asked him to choose between his family and beer; naturally he chose the beer. I heard all this as it happened. It broke my heart to know that dad did not care about us. He said that we were our mother's kids, not his. After hearing this I knew that I did not have a father (he was a womanizer and alcoholic). I hated alcohol as it brought the devil out of people, and if it wasn't for it then probably I could have had a father in the days gone by.

Prickle in a Dream

After a quarrel that lasted over 3 hours between my father and mother, he left home and then no one knew anything about his whereabouts. We waited and thought he would come back as he usually did, but unfortunately we were wrong. I tried looking for him in the nearby villages, but it was all in vain. We were all worried that may be something bad had happened to him.

As we were in the garden about three weeks after his departure, I saw two people walking towards our house. I put down my hoe and decided to go and see who they were. To my surprise, it was my father again, this time not alone, but with some other woman. She was dark-skinned, tall and looked as though she was in her mid 20s.

When he saw me, he asked, "Masembe, where is your mother and everyone else?"

I answered, "They are in the garden."

"Eeh, you mean your mother is still around? I thought she had already left," he said. They entered into the house and he started showing her everything.

He then commanded, "Masembe, go and call everyone else here. Hurry up!"

I ran back to the garden and informed my mother about what was happening. We all held our tools and came back to the house. "From today onwards," he said as he held her closely to himself," this is my new wife. Respect and be loyal to her."

At that point, my mother just went into the house and started yelling out. She couldn't believe what she had just seen or heard. My father and his new wife left with their hands intertwined and promised that they would come back in the evening.

We then also went inside and started comforting our mother. She started telling us her story while shedding more and more tears.

"I grew up in a very poor family. My parents were so poor that they could not afford taking me to school. When I had just turned 16, they decided that I should get married.

So my father got me a man to get married to. He was kind, loving and caring. One day, as he had gone to visit his grandmother in Masaka, the taxi in which he was traveling had an accident and five people including him died instantly. As I was at home, my sisters-in-law came and gave me the shocking news. I felt stunned. I started wondering why it is always the good people who die so early. After the burial I could not take it any further. I could see him in my dreams every day. He became part of my daily thoughts. I badly missed him. He would not leave my mind. I became so thin that my father decided that I should go back home since my husband was already dead.

I stayed at home for a year until my father got me another man to get married to, and that was your father. He was twelve years older than me. He loved me so much at first that we decided to start getting children. On 26 June 1982, we gave birth to you, Mase.

She said this as she pointed at me. "He loved you so much, "she continued, "because he knew that you were going to be his heir. He never wanted anything bad to happen to you. Three years later came our newly born

Prickle in a Dream

baby girl Wanyana. I was mesmerized when I gave birth to you since I wanted a girl child too. Two years later I gave birth to you Mpagi. You were a tiny but sharp young boy who always acted above what your age was. Five years later, I gave birth to you, Seguya." She then got hold of Seguya and placed him on her lap.

"That was where life became so bad for me. Your father hated me ever since that day. I was so helpless; your father resented me and looked at me with so much abhorrence. At one time he even said I was too old for him as though he was any younger. He always echoed that he never gives birth to handicapped children and that I should look for the father of my child." My mother broke down as she ran a memory lane along her past. She cried out on top of her voice as tears also started coming out of our eyes.

"But," she continued, "I loved and praised the Lord more and more for you. I love you so much, Seguya. At least you did not become blind.

It was then that your father started drinking alcohol. He could no longer provide the physical, financial and emotional protection. He started behaving so weirdly. He stopped loving any of us. He even started not coming back home for days and weeks. Lastly, two year later, I gave birth to you Nansubuga, my last born. But I love all of you. You are all my beloved children."

My mother said all this as she was in so much emotional pain. I could sense too much hurt in her eyes. She regretted the day she stepped into my father's house. "But enough is enough, "she continued, "I can't stand being in the same house with another woman."

Then she started gathering all old scraped, ragged clothes and other shabby belongings, rapped them in a very old backcloth and decided that we go and leave her marital home.

Chapter 2

A Journey to Manhood

It was a very hot sunny day at around noon when we set off for our journey. My mother carried our belongings on her head, I carried Seguya on my back as Wanyana, Nansubuga and Mpagi followed us. We moved on empty stomachs since we were not given a chance to prepare anything for ourselves. We moved through rambling forest paths lined by trees with large straggling branches.

We had hardly moved on when Nansubuga started crying out, "Mother, I am hungry!"

As my mother was trying to soothe her, Mpagi shouted, "I am tired of walking. Let's go back home, mother."

My mother replied, "Now my son, we cannot go back home, but wait; we shall reach where we are going."

At that moment, mother pulled out some ripe bananas that she had carried along with her. I never noticed that she had packed anything else apart from our clothes. We sat down for a few minutes, and after eating the bananas, we continued our journey.

After walking for about 1km, I felt I was too tired. I needed to put Seguya down, but the problem was that he couldn't walk. So I told mother we exchange. She carried Seguya, and I carried our belongings.

After walking for some more time, we all felt that we could not continue any further. We were so tired, hungry and so thirsty. We decided to stop and rest for some minutes. As we sat down to take rest, we saw a woman carrying an empty jerry can. My mother stopped her and asked her if there was a well around that place.

"Yes, definitely. That is where I am going," the woman replied.

My mother asked, "Can you please give me your jerry can for some time so that I can fetch some water and give to my children to drink? We are so thirsty and we are still having a very long way to go."

Our piteous state captured the woman's sympathy.

She then said, "This water is not boiled. It has so many germs. May be we go home and I give you safe water. You even look so hungry. You can come to my house and eat something. I have plenty of food there."

It was as if an angel had come down on earth and I just couldn't wait for reaching her home.

She fetched the water and we started following her. We walked a short distance and then we reached her home. We found there three little children who were playing football in their compound. They were all

Prickle in a Dream

hospitable and they knelt down and greeted us all. Barely minutes later, they started calling out my little sisters and brothers to join them in their game. However, my siblings were too tired even to give them a reply. Their mother then invited us into the house, and it was not long before she appeared with plates full of food. She gave everyone enough food and told us that we were even free to ask for more if we needed. We ate the food and, no doubt, it tasted so delicious.

By the time we finished, it had become so dark and we were feeling too weary to continue with our journey. The lady asked us where we were heading to. My mother told her that we had to travel for about fifteen miles more to reach our destination. She then said that it was so risky for us to move at night. So she requested that we spend the night with them and set off for our journey early the next morning. Without hesitation, my mother agreed. She showed us where the shower-rooms were and we took a shower.

Before we met that lady, I thought such good people with pure hearts of gold never existed. She was caring, enthusiastic, kind and pleasant. She made us feel at home.

She offered us one room and it had three beds. I had never slept on a bed in the whole of my life. The room was large and airy. I compared that place with where we were coming from and I regarded that place as heaven. My mother slept with Seguya, I slept with Mpagi and Nansubuga shared her bed with Wanyana. An atmosphere of euphoria surrounded us that night for it was the best sleep ever for us.

At around 6 the next morning, she woke us up telling us that breakfast was ready. She offered us tea and maize. I felt like spending the rest of my life here. After our breakfast, she packed enough maize, yellow bananas, roasted potatoes and a 10 liter-jerry can of water for us. We thanked her so much and she said she was pleased to help us. I carried Seguya and mother carried our belongings. She accompanied us up to the place where she had met us and we continued with our journey.

We moved quite faster this time, since we were refreshed and it was still early enough for the sun to come out. We moved as everyone was praising the good-hearted lady.

It was at that moment that I realized God was always watching over us. He never sleeps nor slumbers. His love for us never fluctuates. I came to believe that I am not just a face in the crowd, but a disciple whom Jesus keeps on loving. His love is so unending.

We moved on and on through mountains, valleys and forests. This time we were all strong and confident since we knew that when we became hungry or thirsty, we had something for the stomach. We stopped at different places and ate something before we finally reached our destination. We walked south of Nakasongola until we reached Luweero District. The land was as dry as a desert. The place looked hotter than the Sahara desert. We moved and crossed to the northern part of the district. The land there was developed from alluvial soil which is deep and is strongly acidic with low organic matter content. The people had small valley dams for the few animals that they reared. They mostly reared hens, pigs, goats and a few had one or two cows. Others had very small plantations but the plants seemed so dry and unhealthy.

Mother then led us to a small village called Butuntumula. After moving for some time, I saw a man coming towards us and welcoming us. He hugged my mother and all of us and then removed the luggage off my mother's head and led us home.

His home had a nice compound with a commodious rhododendron and short trees all over. I really loved what I had seen. I saw a small garden in front of his home and there were banana plantations, potatoes plantations, cassava plantations, avocado trees, jackfruit trees, maize, groundnuts, beans and sugarcanes. I also saw a small kitchen beside his house and it had a strong wooden door. I peeped inside and saw lots of logs lying in the kitchen. I also saw a bicycle beside the kitchen.

He later led us into the idyllic house. He had a small wooden table with three small stools and exquisite mats covered the floor. I also saw that he had two bedrooms and a small store room. He then went into the kitchen and prepared some tea for us. When the tea was ready, he opened the store room and brought out some fried groundnuts which he gave to us to take with the tea. The tea was good and the groundnuts tasted so sweet.

As we were taking the tea, he asked my mother how my father was. My mother started narrating to him the ordeal-stricken experience.
"Actually," she said, "we have come to take refuge here. We have no island of escape."

He agreed that we could stay with him. He offered us one of his bedrooms and that was where the five of us used to sleep all the time we spent at his home. At first, life seemed so fine. He and my mother used to wake up so early in the morning to go to the garden. Since it was a small garden, there was no use for all of us to go to the garden, so my mother suggested that the rest of us stay at home and do the house chores.

There was a small market, a mile away from home, where most people used to sell their products. After harvesting, my uncle would take the products (maize, beans, groundnuts, sweet potatoes, etc.) to the market and sell them there.

Using the money he earned, he offered to pay for my school fees. Although in my former school I was in primary five, uncle got me a new school and asked that I joined primary seven. As luck could have it, I was admitted to primary seven. He bought me four books for all the four subjects that we used to study and a pen. Just as in my first school, most pupils in this school also never owned uniforms and shoes. The school was far away from home and I used to wake up so early in the morning and walked till I reached school. I was so bright and teachers used to like me immensely. I finished my PLE (Primary Leaving Exams) and I got a first grade. I was the only one who got a first grade in the whole school. Since the school had never got any first grade in its history, the Headmaster was extremely happy with me, so he offered to pay for my secondary education (Ordinary level of education). I studied and finished my Ordinary level of education but still had to overcome another struggle to attain the Advanced level of education.

Meanwhile my mother involved herself in all sorts of odd jobs to acquire some money to send me and my siblings to school. She tendered people's gardens, cleaned people's homes, weaved baskets and would sell them around the village. This, however, did not raise enough money for us to go to good schools. So she enrolled my siblings into village schools. Nevertheless, she always felt a bit relieved. Indeed it was better to live in a house with less food, but enough peace and love.

She also decided that we leave my uncle's place and get a house for rent, cheap enough to remain within our means. My uncle helped us look for a single rental room in the next village at five thousand Uganda shilling per month. My mother paid for three months and we started staying there.

That was when I came to realize that the saying "Man the breadwinner/woman the caretaker," had no significance in our family, since it was only the woman who played both roles in our lives. She did all sorts of jobs to give me and my siblings a good upbringing, something far different from what she had for herself. Despite her illiteracy, she did everything possible for her to see us in school.

As time went by, life became so hard for us all. Mother started becoming sick and weaker so that she could no longer manage to do the work she used to do. She caught diarrhea that lasted more than a week and a dry cough which usually worsened in the evenings. She had a hideous, unexplained fatigue, she continually experienced memory loss, depression and neurological disorders, and she rapidly lost her weight and caught unusual blemishes on the tongue.

At the tender age of fifteen, I had become the bread winner of the family. Mother had become so frail, sickly and senile. The mantle of taking care of my siblings fell on me as I was the eldest and, to tell the truth, this was not any easy task. This was when I came to the realization that I was no longer a small boy who needed only to sit down and everything would be brought to him on a silver plate. It was absolutely clear that I had a big load already on my shoulders and that my mother's health and my siblings' education depended entirely on me. I did not have to sit on my laurels; I had to be quick and plan a lot.

"Mase, my dear son, we do not have any source of income; nor do we have any food. I would have loved to work so hard to put food on the table for you my children, but the illness has hit me so hard that I am so frail and I cannot do anything. Let me use this opportunity while I still can, to tell you this; I am leaving your siblings in your hands. Mase, Mase, you are not lame; I want you to be hardworking and courageous."

"But mother, why you are saying all these . . .?" I stammered.

"Let me finish, my son. This may be the last chance I have to tell you all these things. If I still live, then you, my children, are the only reason why remain alive. Mase, please take good care of your siblings, especially Seguya. Always encourage him. I may not have given you the best, but believe me, I tried. I know that life has so many opportunities for you. I know you will be a strong and prosperous person; always remember to ask

God to guide you in each and everything. Never abandon any of your siblings."

I could not make out why mother said all those things to me then. I knew she was sick but I could not imagine it was her time to leave us. Not at this time, I said to myself. For the first time in a long time, I felt my inner voice reassure me; I was so optimistic about the whole situation. For some reason I knew God would not let my mother die. I prayed like never before, and I had the strong conviction that God would come to my rescue because we could not even afford to buy any more medicine for mother.

The situation was so demanding and sometimes I cried and wept but at the end of the day, nothing really changed. Whenever I cried, I would usually hide myself away from my siblings. I would never allow them to see me crying because if they saw me, they would not be inspired to become better. It could only dampen their spirits and I wanted them to believe in themselves, even when the going was tough.

I always believed that the ability to change their situation was solely in their hands and so since they were disadvantaged from the very beginning, they should learn to endure and have that mental ability. This was not easy at all, but I thank God since, with time, they started hardening, believing in themselves and understanding that poverty was the mindset and that with handwork they could overcome it.

I would wake up very early in the morning, just to make sure everything was in place. I would come out of bed at around four, prepare breakfast, wash utensils and try to put everything in the house in order, in preparation for the day.

At around the age of 5, I would wake up my siblings to prepare for school since their school was about eight kilometers away from home. I would give them breakfast and they could all set off as a group for school. I would head back home to check on mum, who spent most of her time in bed. I would then prepare lunch for her, wait for a council who usually spent the day with her to come and I would finally leave for school at around 11:00am.

Over the weekends, I would tender people's gardens and cleaned people's homes in order to raise some money for rent. It would have been good if I was paid all the money I worked for, but most of the people I worked for kept on promising to pay me day after the other, until I could just let it go. It hurt me so much to work without pay, until I stopped working for them.

One day, on her sickbed, mother called me. "I have always seen you as . . . "(cough) "a very . . ." (cough) "hardworking . . . Harrummph!" She said this and then she gestured for some water. I hastily went to the pot, poured some water in a mug and came back with it. As I handed over the mug of water to my mother, Nansubuga, bumped in.

"Mase, I have made some money. We can buy some medicine for mother," she said innocently as she handed me some coins.

"But where did you get this money from?" I asked.

"I always help Jaja to fetch water. Today her son came from Kampala and found me helping her out and he gave me this money," she proudly replied.

I counted the money and it was seven hundred shillings. I was so impressed. This money wasn't enough to buy mother's medicine, but the way Nansubuga acquired it and the fact that, instead of her buying sweets like girls of her age would do, she brought it safely home to buy medicine for mother made me so emotional and astonished. This little girl always helped a certain lady known to many as "jaja". She had four sons and they all lived in Kampala. She always had enough to eat because her sons brought her grocery every month, but she was too old to do anything on her own. Nansubuga and other children always helped her to fetch water, make the fire, cook food and wash clothes and she would in turn give them food to eat and her blessings. I remember that Nansubuga once told me that jaja had blessed her to become the richest woman in the village and that she believed it would come to pass one day.

With that little token from Jaja's son, we were able to buy mother some tablets from the only clinic in the whole village. I had to run as fast as I could until I came back with the medicine. I then silently said to myself: "I have to look for all sorts of jobs to get some money to look after my mother."

We were living in complete penury and destitution. I had to fight tooth and nail to reverse the situation. I knew I was the only knight in shining armor that my family had. I straight away started to look for a job. I went to a place where they made bricks. A friend of mine had told me that they needed some porters there. I was more than willing to do any job as long as it brought food on the table. As I approached the place, I met a handicapped lady trying to lift some luggage to earn some money. This opened up my mind and reminded me of what mother had said to me. I increased my pace for I was too eager to get something to do for a penny. In a jiffy, I had reached the place. It was such a busy area. All the workers there looked so strong. As I looked around, my eyes met a certain man at the corner who I later leant was their supervisor. His beady eyes rolled in their sockets like those of a doll. He had such a mean look. He looked so unfriendly but this did not deter me from inquiring whether he had a place for me. I would look a fool if I left the place without saying anything. I stood at a distance, organized, and fastened my dirty brown shirt, yawned a bit, cleared my throat and then gathered the courage to say something.

"Good evening . . . sir."

"What are you here for?" he blurted out.

His voice was very hard and so cold. I wondered how a simple greeting would be returned by such a bitter and callous question. I knew this was not going to be easy but all the same, I had to try out my luck.

"Do you need any help, here?" I frightfully mumbled.

"Yes, of course, we do need a lot of help," he replied with a grinning smile on his face.

I felt a rush of excitement run through my veins for I knew I would get some money to feed my family. I looked at him critically and noticed that his right hand had six fingers. Could it be the reason why he was so proud and arrogant?

"So, where do I . . . " I asked, trying to find the right words to use lest the boss changed his mind.

"Sir, how many should we put on the first level?" interrupted one of the workers.

"Idiot! How many times do you want me to tell you about the same thing? If I must repeat, then it should be for the very last time. Do you understand?" the supervisor retorted.

"Yes, sir," the worker hastily replied.

"Put 5 by 6 on the first level, then 5 by 5 on the next level, then 5 by 4, 5 by 3, and so on and so forth . . . understood?" The supervisor shouted angrily.

"Exactly, sir," the worker humbly replied.

"Good. What are you still doing here? Get back to work," the supervisor commanded him.

I kept wondering how much money the boys were receiving. They did a lot of work, yet their boss had the ferocity of a lion. They must have been as desperate as I was because the working conditions were not favorable at all.

"So what do I start with?" I said, bearing in mind that the man must have forgotten I was standing right in front of him.

"If you want to work, you can come. We need help, but you only come because you want to help and do not expect any payment. You can work, but who is going to pay you?" he said as he sternly looked at me critically to see what my reaction would be.

I could not believe what this man had said. It was not until I noticed the sarcasm in his hoarse voice that I realized that the world is not always fair. I wondered if other workers were not paid too. I was so disappointed that I went away without saying any single word.

I walked back home, so miserable and dejected.

At School, things were not any better, since I continually went late due to my responsibilities at home. I lagged behind in every aspect, from syllabus coverage to knowledge of the different subjects. I fell among the last performers in class. Although my teachers understood my plight and tried as much as they could to help, things were not getting better. I had taken up a lot of responsibility, and so my mind was very much preoccupied making me unable to concentrate much in class.

I usually had worries about mum's health, rent, food and the safety of my siblings as they went to school. The thought of finding school fees for them continuously howled like a banshee in my head. We were down and out for the whole period when mother was sick.

Although some times the parish priest helped in paying school fees for my siblings, I usually had to take care of the other responsibilities in the house.

Fortunately, Mr. Kawooya, the headmaster, was a very kind man and used to always take me as his own son. He understood the situation my siblings and I were going through, so I rarely paid fees. Whenever the going got tough, Mr. Kawooya was my refuge. He always counseled me as his own son and I loved the hugs he used to give me. I felt loved all the time I spent in his school. I always had someone to fall back to whenever I got any problem. Whenever I would not be so busy, I would go and help out in his farm as a way of showing my gratitude.

Chapter 3

THE RAINY SEASON

Oh dear, I soundly slept in the classroom, saliva was dipping from the side of my month on to the desk and finally down on to the ground. In a couple of minutes a big pool of saliva had already formed on the floor. Though deep in the slumber land, my stomach was grumbling frequently. I had had no lunch that day at school since my meal card had not been given to me for I had not completed my school fees.

Suddenly, I received a heavy slap on my left cheek. Mr. Munyagwa, the no-nonsense mathematics teacher, had quietly come in for his afternoon lesson and found that the whole class had focused its attention on me, instead of reading their books and concentrating on something constructive. Out of the blue, I woke up almost falling off the desk, as the heavy slap had caught me unawares. On opening my eyes, I caught sight of the teacher, but anger, rage and fear had so engulfed me that when I stood, I was so motionless, and I was perplexed.

It was then that I heard a soft voice trying to wake me up, "Mase!, Masembe!" my frail mother cried out, "wake up . . .,Wake up, the water is getting into the house."

All the while I was deep asleep, and it had been raining cats and dogs. The water had started finding its way into the house. The sight of this made me quiver with rage. I then quickly jumped off the mat on which I used to sleep. At that time I could see panic in my mother's eyes and I regretted that I could not do much to save the situation.

I then called my siblings and instructed them to gather our property so that we could be able to fasten them up on the roof. We then got hold of all the containers we had in the house which comprised of sizeable cups, bowls and saucepans, and started drawing the water out, thus preventing a smalllake from forming in the house. I stationed Wanyana next to the door, and Mpagi, and Nansubuga inside the house to fetch out the dirty water that had crawled inside the house. Since our latrines were built way high above the ground, I had to carry mother and Seguya to the latrine steps. I then got hold of the hoe and started digging trenches to carry the water away. This was not an easy task because I did all this while it was still raining on my head. I looked in the neighborhood and everyone was busy trying to draw the water out of their houses. People's compounds became waterlogged and the situation was so unbearable. One could not easily cross over from one place to another.

We had always been hearing stories of people drowning in their houses as a result of heavy downpour and over sleeping. After some good time, I realized that the rain had come down in intensity until it finally stopped. I then decided to check on my old strapless watch and it indicated that it was already 5am in the morning. We continued drawing the water out of the house until it was completely drawn.

We did not go to school that day since we had to check on the damages the rains had caused to us. During the latter part of the day, our family tried to clean the house, and washed the water-soaked clothes and mud-spattered items. We put them in the sunshine to dry thus removing the foul smell from the house.

At around 4pm that day, the elders, as it was their custom whenever such a disaster occurred, called for a village meeting to ascertain the incurred losses of people and property.

Since my mother was too weak to attend, I went and represented our family. Many People reported that their houses had collapsed. This was due to age and the poor materials used during construction. Those who delayed to wake up lost most of their belongings due to too much water. The market became waterlogged and one could hardly pass there. The elders wrote down whatever was reported and then released us.

As I had just reached home, the parish priest appeared.

"I heard about the calamity that happened in this village of yours last night. Did it affect any of you?" he inquired.

"We are all somehow safe," I replied.

"Good. So how is mother? I have taken some good time without setting my eyes on her in church. Is she alright?" he asked as he stepped near our doorway.

"Mother is terribly sick; she can scarcely eat anything and she has a high fever," I replied as the priest stepped into the house. On entering the house, he found my mother cuddled on her old small wooden bed. She was shuddering from head to toe.

"You mean it has all come to this?" he said as he tried to lift up my mother. Her temperature was too high and she was too weak since she had refused to take anything for the past two days.

He then instructed me to get her some better clothes and told me that we were going to hospital. He held my mother's left hand as he slowly led her into his old Volkswagen. My mother and I occupied the back seat as he sat in the driver's seat and drove us off. We traveled several kilometers until we finally reached the county hospital located in the far East of the district.

The nurses ran towards the vehicle and took her inside. They asked us what she was suffering from and I told them that it was malaria.

After several tests and observations, the doctor concluded that she was HIV positive. Whoa! I quivered and wished it was a nightmare, but it wasn't. I then told the doctor to reexamine her and he told us that that would be after two months. Since her condition was appalling, she was admitted in the hospital.

At that moment, the priest decided to go back home and come along with Wanyana who would manage to take good care of her. They returned several minutes later with fruits, boiled water, food and some of her clothes. She stayed in the hospital and I went back home.

These became more trying moments for us all. I became more worried about everything. My siblings could cry day and night since mother was missing. I would wake up so early, prepare breakfast for my siblings, prepare them for school, make the food to be taken to the hospital, and then run to the hospital before finally going to school. I told Mpagi and Nansubuga to prepare food to take to the hospital in the evening since they used to leave school earlier. The teachers and fellow students isolated me because of the many problems that always surrounded me. Life became so unbearable and meaningless to me.

The priest would pass by the hospital every evening to check on her. He even announced in church that my mother was admitted in Nakaseke hospital, so several people from the congregation used to come and this comforted us. He also paid our outstanding rental charges for three months and completed my siblings' school fees for that term.

After a period of three weeks, her condition became better, so she was finally discharged from the hospital. She came back home and we took good care of her until she was finally in good health. She even started doing her odd jobs again. Once in a while, the priest would visit us, pray with us and encourage us.

Mother worked so hard. Although the money was not all that much, little by little it added up to something and she started saving. She also started taking her woven baskets to the market to boost her sales. As time went by, she deserted the other jobs and concentrated mostly on the baskets. However, the market was too far away from home and she couldn't manage walking there every day, so she decided to rent a house nearer to the market. It was a very busy market and I later got to know that it was not a long distance from this place to Kampala. We got a room near the market. It was made of brick and bigger than the one we had originally stayed in.

My mother's sales increased and I also managed to finish my A' level though it was a great hustle. Mother even started purchasing vegetables and selling them at some little profit. When she was back on her feet, she managed to buy herself a cheap phone since she wanted to stay in close communication with her customers.

One hot afternoon in the month of March, as we were busy at home trying to finalize with a few baskets, mother received a phone call from someone who introduced herself as my father's mistress. She said that dad had collapsed and been taken to hospital but he died an hour later and that his body lay in Mulago hospital mortuary. He had died a few hours after he was admitted to this hospital, irreparably damaged by alcohol-related diseases. She told us that the corpse was to be taken to the village for burial.

We then swiftly prepared ourselves and left for the village. On our way, mother, and all my siblings cried endlessly. I forced tears to come out of my eyes, but they were as dry as a desert.

This brought back all my memories about my father. Memories of him are complex, multi-stranded, and perhaps unreliable with the passing of time. To a great extent, they are the worst, yet to some degree, I come to think that he was a very intelligent and bright man, since he always managed to get top jobs in different banks. It makes me sad to see what alcohol had turned him into and to realize the fact that it was the cause of his death.

My father was always at bars, drinking and gambling. It was this, and having a number of mistresses, that made it impossible for him to support us. He neglected all his roles as a father. A father's role in a child's life is indispensable and very important in helping to facilitate the healthy development of a child. A father in essence is the role model of a boy child and has been given the pedestal of leadership in the home; he is always seen as a keeper and leader of his family. However, I missed all this from my father. I realized that I never had a father in all my life. I only had a mother; that's why I have always been thankful for having a mother who managed to give me twice the love and support to make up for my absent father.

We reached home and nothing much had changed since we left. We found so many people gathered in our small compound and many cried endlessly, as others kept on arriving from far away areas. As we were moving, I could see people pointing fingers at me and my siblings whispering out sentences like, "you are the one who has been asking for the whereabouts of the orphans, see . . . they have arrived."

We went inside the house and our father's body was lying in the middle of the house, wrapped in black cloth. There were around fifteen women and one man sitting inside the house. Whenever someone came in, one woman would uncover the face of my father to allow him/her to set his eyes on the deceased for the last time. My siblings and mother wept loudly when they set their eyes on my father's body.

At around 4pm, we were told to go and gather at the burial grounds, where my father was going to be buried.

"Good afternoon all of you!" the clan elder said as we all gathered to the burial grounds to bury our father. "We are very sorry for the loss of our dear friend, son, father and uncle. He was a very hardworking, loving and caring man. I think we all know that. The Bible tells us in Ecclesiastes chapter 3, that there is a time for everything, a time to be born and a time to die. May be his time for dying had reached. May his soul rest in eternal peace! As you all know, the deceased has left so many children and wives. So at this moment, I request all the widows and orphans to stand up on their feet so that we can see them."

After I had stood up, I saw five women and sixteen (16) children standing up. I wondered where all these women and children had come from.

He then continued, "Number 1 has 5 children," He said as he looked at my mother, "Number 2 has 3 children, number 3 has 5 and number 4 has only one child and wife number 5 has 2 children."

I looked at all the other children, two of whom resembled Mpagi and number 2's first born was just two years younger than me. I wondered why father had never told anyone that he had such grown up children elsewhere.

"But since the clan does not have enough money to take care of the children, and nor did the deceased leave anything for them, all the widows are expected to go with their children and look after them. You may look at this land and think it was his . . . No, this land on which he built his house is just an ancestral land; so it belongs to the clan. If any of the orphans or widows is willing to stay in for some time, it is okay as long as he/she does not take it for good, but there are some of his belongings that you are all going to share just after this," he concluded.

We were led through some dirges and prayers by the priest of that village. My father was lowered into his grave and then we were allowed to put some soil to cover him. As we left the burial grounds, I could hear several women whispering to each other, "The man had so many children! Imagine all those 16, and they are all still young. At least he could have left some assets for their mothers to take care of the children."

As we went into the house, the clan head pulled out some two kanzus, five shirts and two pairs of trousers. He handed one kanzu to me, and he divided up the remaining attires to all the sons of the deceased. The girls did not receive anything. The clan head again told all the widows to take care of their own children.

After burial, we came back home and continued with our daily schedule. When my mother's profits had accumulated, she decided I should join an institute to continue with my education, since she never had enough money to finance me at the university. I enrolled for Bachelor of Arts (Arts) since it was one of the cheapest courses offered. This institute was only about five hundred meters away from home. This made it possible for me to commute to the institute every day. However this did not stop me from working hard at school.

Flying had been a lifelong dream of mine, and I had decided at an early age that I wanted to be a pilot when I grew up. Life, however, made a drastic change and I had to live far away from my dream. The expenses involved in attaining the qualification gave me no choice, so I never got any closer to this elusive dream.

With this course I had started on, my aims changed. I started looking into the direction of being a social worker because of one of the course units I was offered. But I dropped out before I could finalize my course.

However, before I could finish up with this course, mother started acquiring an on and off fever until she finally became bed-ridden. I had to leave school in order to take good care of her. Mpagi stayed at home with me as all the others went to school. I used to buy her painkillers but they would not do much. She would feel pain when swallowing, lost her appetite and felt extreme fatigue. Coughing, nausea, abdominal cramps, severe persistent diarrhea, vomiting, and severe headaches became part of her life. She always experienced mental confusion and forgetfulness and lost a lot of weight. She seemed so weak and her face was pale. One look at her will make anyone suspect that she had been sick for the last century. She was wallowing in dire pain. Taking sleeping pills was her only island of escape. I felt she was living on borrowed time.

After five months or so of such a terrible quandary, she called me, held my right arm and in a whisper-like tone said "Masembe, I don't think I will live any longer. I am too tired and need to rest." As she spoke all this to me, I could see her body in too much pain. It was the first time in life that I saw mother so scared and sad and I saw endless tears trickling down her emaciated chin.

"Take good care of your siblings and love them as I have always loved you. Even at the hardest of times never ever part ways with them." She continued.

She then slowly released my hand and closed her eyes forever. "Mother, wait!" I cried out, and then all of a sudden felt lost for words. I went silent for a while and swiftly shouted to her again "mother!" I tried to shake her, but she couldn't even whisper any other word. I forced her eyes open, but they would immediately close themselves. I called her loudly, but she seemed not to hear my voice anymore.

I became so devastated. "Mother, now what is this you are doing to me?" I screamed. At that time I was only sixteen years, Wanyana was thirteen, Mpagi was eleven, Seguya was six and Nansubuga was only four years old. I felt as if my world had reached its end. Mpagi and I then started crying out at the top of our voices so that people in the market started coming and gathering in the house. One of them quickly ran out and brought my siblings. I could hear their loud lamentations even before they reached home. The world turned so dark and I couldn't hold the sight of all this; so I decided to leave the room.

This dingy day is indelibly registered in my mind. I can hardly forget what mother did and said to me before she died. Her passing away was a permanent, shaping influence in my life and maturity. It forced me to grow up much quicker than I would have under normal circumstances. Growing up became an uphill battle for me and my siblings. Life lost its rhythm and old pattern at that moment.

I realized that I had to become the father and mother to my siblings. I realized mother had gone on a journey so far away and never to return. My siblings cried day and night. They would cry whenever they would set their eyes on any of my mother's clothes. I would counsel them, but it was always hard for me since I would also end up shedding tears in front of them.

I felt as if I could not take life anymore; I was completely in a daze. I was so depressed and completely drained with the loss of my mother. She was a teacher, friend, provider, comforter, listener, disciplinarian, caregiver and the sole breadwinner. I loved everything about my mother. She was the best in the whole world, a replica of an angel.

Chapter 4

THE HUSH TIMES

In Africa, after the death of the parents, children are left at the mercy of relatives. Relatives do divide the orphans among themselves. Ours was, however, a different case, since we got the chance to be taken up by one particular maternal uncle. It was at this uncle's place that we had lived before we moved to the small rented house. This wasn't bad at all as it could give us the chance to grow up together without being separated from relatives. I also thought it was a good idea since we had once stayed with him and he had always acted humanely all the days that we spent there.

"Get into the car. We do not have more time to waste here. I have to meet some business partners today at Serena. We shall have to first go to your former house and collect your belongings, and then head home," Uncle said as he opened the door to the driver's seat of his Mercedes Benz.

As I struggled to open the car door, he jumped off his seat, "You lift it like this, and then it will be open . . . " he said as he illustrated.

Prickle in a Dream

After we had entered, he fastened the car door, climbed on to his own seat and we set off. As we progressed, I kept on looking outside. I saw people of different sizes and ages walking along the road. At one point, I saw a pregnant woman, carrying a young baby on her back and a heavy load on her head. As I leaned back in the comfortable and elegant conveyance, I pondered again about the love my mother had for us. Thoughts about my father too reappeared, but they were not as pleasing or warm as those about mother. I never received any love from him and I could enjoy the love of mother for only a very limited time.

Finally we reached home. Uncle quickly instructed us to collect our belongings and put them into the car. We packed our belongings in different polythene bags as quickly as a dog can lick a dish, and we finally left for his place.

"We are now real orphans.' I wonder how we are going to live without mother," I thought as Nansubuga tried to tickle me saying, "Mase, look at this very long building." She pointed out a very broad tower against the sky with a tapered galaxy of lights and asked, "How did they construct it?"

"Wanyana, look, there are two levels of road here. Don't you think we may slide off and fall down?" wondered Mpagi as we passed via the Northern bypass.

I saw several supermarkets, meeting points, petrol stations and trading centers on the way. There were a few pedestrians on the roads. Most people traveled in their own vehicles or used commuter taxis. Several poorly-maintained motorcycles locally known as Boda bodas transported different people through the rush hour traffic as drivers of commuter taxis continued throwing vulgar words to them. "Look at this fool! Where did he learn driving from?" one commuter taxi driver angrily shouted at a boda boda cyclist as he tried to fix himself in a very small passage.

"Hello . . . Hello . . . Yes, I am coming. Just give me a few minutes from now. I will be right there," Uncle spoke on his phone.

As far as I could see, we had reached a place known as kololo. I could see several signposts reading "Kololo family supermarket," "one-in-all discotheque Kololo," "Kololo lane apartments," etc. All I knew was that the place was located in Kampala since we had studied about the Kololo Airstrip and the Tank hill in my p.3 class in a subject called Social Studies. I remembered the teacher emphasizing that Kololo was located in Kampala. Very big houses were scattered all over the region. I felt as though we were in a different world from that in which we were living. It looked more populous, more picturesque and more stirring.

As we continued, uncle branched off to the parking lot of a very big shop which I later got to know was a supermarket. As he went in, he told us to open the car doors to let in some fresh air. I could see little children coming out of the supermarket with their parents as they held ice cream cones, of vanilla and chocolate flavors, and cakes. We all sat in the car and wished uncle could come with a dish of ice cream for all of us too. After a few minutes, he reappeared with several polythene bags containing two loaves of bread, a tin of margarine, packets of milk, sugar and rice and a bottle of tomato sauce. He quickly put them in the car and drove off.

About ten minutes later we reached a very big fenced house with a green metallic gate. Uncle first stepped out, pressed a switch, which I later learnt was for the bell, and instantly one young girl came and opened a pair of gates. We passed through, and the gates clashed

Prickle in a Dream

behind us. The car stopped at the front door of the house.

Two large dogs sat demurely in the compound. There were two bungalow houses inside the fence. I later came to know that one of them was referred to as the main house and the other, a boys-quarter. Both houses looked so stunning.

"Is this really going to be our new home? It looks so beautiful! I think it is the best place I have ever been to," I thought.

I looked at the gate once again, then at the bow-shaped aluminum windows and doors and finally looked around the compound. The compound was beautiful with flowers and grasses all over.

"Welcome back home, Daddy," said the young girl as she ran towards the driver's seat.

Uncle replied as he stepped out and gave a peck on the little girl's chubby cheek, "Thank you my dear. How has been your day?"

"Daddy, I have already finished my homework," the little girl replied with a winning smile on her face.

"That's good. Now you go inside and tell Sharifah to come and remove this from the car." He said as he hurriedly stepped back from the car.

"Sharifahh! Sharifah!. . . Daddy has said . . ." she called out as she entered into the house.

A dark-skinned woman, who appeared to be in her late 20s, appeared and started removing the supermarket commodities from the car. Uncle asked us to remove our belongings and take them into the house.

"Helloooo, five minutes sir . . . yesss! Yes sir," he spoke so loudly on the phone.

"Sharifah, tell Mummy to get them one of the free rooms in the house and make them comfortable. They are going to start staying with us. I am rushing somewhere and I will come in the evening," he said as he slammed the door and instantly left.

"You are all welcome. How are you?" she warmly welcomed us.

"Wiiiya aoorite thank you Aunt!" Nansubuga hurriedly answered as we all laughed out loud.

"I was busy in the kitchen and I think the food I was preparing could be burning. Let me take your belongings into your room as you enter there. I will come back and greet you."

I carried Seguya as the rest followed me and we all entered the sitting room and everything there dazzled me. The furniture, the red woolen carpet and the round glass table there looked so gorgeous. I looked around and there were so many toys scattered around. I felt blissful, because I was sure my siblings would love playing with all of them. Before they even settled down, Nansubuga rushed for the big doll on the floor, Seguya for the toy car and Mpagi for the toy train.

"Wanyana, this baby is crying she needs milk." Nansubuga told Wanyana as she lifted up the doll that was now making baby-like cries.

I also saw a huge television in one of the corners of the sitting room switched on, although no one appeared watching it. In the other corner was a well-varnished wooden piece having portraits of all the family members. I finally settled down and felt very comfortable as I sat in those leather chairs.

Wanyana and I focused our eyes on the television, and then Sharifah reappeared, "I am sorry I had to leave you here alone"she said.

"No, it is okay, where are aunt and the children?" I asked.

"They are all sleeping. Whenever they finish taking their lunch, they go to bed and rest. It is only today

Prickle in a Dream

that Esther delayed to sleep. You will see Ernest and Elijah in the evening when they wake up. They are all still young. Esther is the oldest of all and she has just turned 12, Ernest and Elijah are 8 and 6 respectively," she said.

"Esther? Which Esther are you talking about?"

"Esther is the little girl who opened the gate for you when you got here. Didn't you see her?"

"Oh yes! I saw her."

"Is this station broadcasting interesting things for you?" She asked as she held the remote and turned to a different station.

She quickly went to where Seguya was, "How are you?" she said as she offered her hand to him. She then went to Nansubuga and carried her on her lap as she smiled and welcomed her.

"But you and she resemble each other," she said as she pointed at Wanyana. "I welcome you all here. I hope you are fine. I believe you have had a tedious drive. I understand how Daddy can drive when in a hurry. By the way, I am so sorry for the loss of your parents. Don't worry, life will be better."

She sounded so calm, good, compassionate, and loving. She later vanished and came back with a plate of cool, sliced pineapple.

"You can share this as I go and prepare evening tea," she said as she left for the kitchen.

The pineapple tasted so delicious. As we were still enjoying the sweetness, a beautiful tall lady appeared.

"What are you doing? See what you have done to my sitting room! Pineapple everywhere . . . Look! Even flies have started entering into the house. Where have you come from, where you do not know that pineapple juice attracts flies? By the way, who told you to eat them from inside? Pineapple should only be eaten from the kitchen, not here. Have you heard?" she shouted.

"We are sorry, aunt," Wanyana quickly replied.

"Sorry for yourselves. You are all so foolish," she snarled, "now go and get a bucket of water and start scrubbing my carpet. I want it clean."

"Aunt, we are going to clean it very properly," said Mpagi.

"You better do so as fast as possible," she replied.

At that moment, I envisaged only aloofness and stiffness from her. She needn't have treated us like that the first time we met her, even if we had made a mistake. She never even gave us a chance to greet her and nor did she welcome us to their home.

I was stupefied, numb, and half out of my skin from the cold and threatening voice. I was so scared that I could not move even the smallest muscle in my body. Minutes later I regained my composure and went to the kitchen where she and Sharifah were to show me where the mop and cleaning sponge were.

"No! I will clean there. Do not worry! You are still visitors" Sharifah said.

"So . . . have you come back empty handed?" she shouted at me.

"Mummy! We have woken up," Elijah and some other two children, a boy and a girl, said as they walked towards their mother. When I looked at them I recognized them to be Ernest and Esther according to what Sharifah had earlier told us.

She looked at them, smiled and said, "Okay, now go to sharifah and tell her to give you pineapple."

"No, mummy, I do not want pineapple, I want juice," Esther said.

"Okay, go and tell her whatever you want and she will give you," aunt replied.

She quickly wore a pale look as the children left, and stared at me with the ferocity of an infuriated lion.

Prickle in a Dream

"Aunt, Sharifah has said that she will clean it," I told her.

"Is she the one who has dirtied it? Go out, turn to your left. You will see the bathroom. Pick all the cleaning facilities there and start cleaning it," she roared.

I quickly went, came back with Wanyana and directed her how to clean the carpet.

At around 6pm, uncle came back. He entered into the sitting room, kissed his wife on the cheek, put his briefcase in the sofas, slackened his tie and then finally settled down. After everyone had finished greeting him, he told Esther to go and call Sharifah.

"Welcome back, sir," Sharifah said.

"Thank you. Aaah, have you prepared a room for our visitors?" he asked.

"Yes sir! The second room in the boys-quarter," Sharifah replied.

"Good! Now you can go," he told her.

She vanished and then came back, "Daddy, the tea is ready," she said.

Uncle quickly told all of us to go to the dining room and take our evening tea. We all sat on the dining table and we were all served milk, buttered-bread and fried eggs.

After taking the tea, Esther said that she wanted to get back to the sitting room.

"You can now go back and watch the TV, and I think we have some very good movie here which you can watch. I am very sure you will all like them," Uncle said as he stood up to go and check the movies. We followed him to the sitting room. He hastily selected one and then played it. It was a very good movie and we surely liked it. Uncle also sat down for a few minutes and after seeing the smiles on our faces, he rose up to go to the bathroom.

"I think you are all enjoying it, so let me first go and take a bath. I will come back later," he said as he stood up to go to his bedroom.

"The food is ready. Please stand up and join the others on the dining table," Sharifah said before we could finish watching the interesting movie.

We reached the table and a rich aroma enraptured our noses. On top of 11 plates and glasses, there were two big plates, one having matoke and the other rice, a very big dish containing beef, a big jar of passion fruit juice and a small dish containing cabbages. I and my siblings sat comfortably looking at everyone else getting a plate and serving themselves. We stayed inert in our seats until uncle said, "Let each one of you pick a plate and put some food before it gets so cold."

"But you people you never cease to amaze me. Now who are you waiting for to serve you? Are you waiting for your caretaker? It is okay, continue waiting," aunt interrupted.

I promptly stood up, served food on five plates and then handed each of my siblings a plate of food. All my siblings ate until they were as full as a tick.

After everyone else had finished eating, I poured juice in all the glasses and gave them out. After having supper, uncle told Sharifah to show us our bedroom. We moved out of the main house, turned to the left and we were led to a big bedroom containing three big wooden beds. I looked at the beds and they all had big mattresses, cushions, white bed sheets and squared blankets. I looked at the wall.

"I think all of you can share these three beds. If you get any problem, you can call me. I sleep in the next room on your left . . . By the way, there are bathrooms on your right in case you want to take a bath," she said as she

Prickle in a Dream

stepped out. "So where do all the others sleep?" Mpagi asked her as she left.

She stopped and said, "They all sleep in the main house. It has five bedrooms. One is shared by Mummy and Daddy whereas Esther, Ernest and Elijah all sleep in different rooms. The fifth one is a visitors' room. Infact I had organized for you that one, but mummy said it was better for you to take up this one."

"It is okay. It is also a nice room," Mpagi said.

"I hope you like it," she said as she quickly vanished.

I looked at all my siblings and I could sense the happiness all of them felt. We all went to the bathroom, one after the other. I entered there first and there were a big bath tab, a big white towel, a piece of soap and a soft sponge. I enjoyed the warm clean bath. I never wanted to leave the bathroom.

Wanyana shared the bed with Nansubuga, Mpagi and I shared another while we left Seguya to sleep alone. Nansubuga displayed an enormous smile as she led us through the prayers. Wanyana, Seguya and Mpagi also seemed very comfortable as they went to their beds.

All my siblings looked as happy as a flea in a doghouse. Life seemed so good and beautiful as I enjoyed the soft, warm and comfortable bed.

But barely a week after the death of our mother, everything changed in a blink of an eye. It was the birth of all the hard and tough new times in our world.

The next morning, Sharifah woke up early and went to the kitchen. I suddenly woke up as well, walked to the kitchen and found her preparing breakfast. I asked her if I should help out on anything.

"No, don't mind. I am only preparing breakfast; then I will prepare the children to school."

When she had put everything on the table, she woke up Esther, Elijah and Ernest to prepare them for school. As they were taking breakfast, uncle walked in slowly as his wife tried to fasten his tie.

"Hurry up. I am going to be so late for work. The problem is it is a Monday morning and so too much traffic jam," he told his children.

"We are tired of working for you and you just come and eat. Starting from tomorrow, all of you are expected to wake up at around 5am and help Sharifah with some work. You will be washing the clothes and utensils as she prepares the children to go to school," aunt said after her husband and the children had left.

That night as I was still sleeping, mother appeared to me. She was dressed in a white negligee and she looked so beautiful. She came and sat next to me and started whispering to me in a very soft and humble voice.

"Mase, please take good care of your siblings." She said.

"Mother! Where have you been? I have always been looking for you everywhere but I was unable to see you. We are now staying in Kampala. Life is so far good. Seguya is . . ."

As I was still speaking, she disappeared. All of a sudden I opened my eyes and realized it was a dream. I turned on my left and right; the only people I could see around were my siblings. It was too hard to believe it was a dream. Before I could get another round of sleep, someone knocked and suddenly opened the door. It was Sharifah again, "Mase, you mean you are already awake? Aunt had told me to wake you and your siblings up to start washing the clothes," she said as she moved out.

I could hardly deem what she had said to me. I looked like a deer caught in the headlights. I was shocked by Sharifah's words. I quickly left my bed, looked outside

Prickle in a Dream

and it looked so dark. I suddenly went to the sitting room, looked at the clock, and it was 5 in the morning. This really perplexed me. I went to the bathroom, collected all the dirty clothes of everyone in the house and started washing them. Sharifah prepared breakfast, set the children for school, and later washed the utensils. At around 7am, aunt woke up, walked around the whole house, found me washing in the bathroom and greeted me. She later went to the kitchen and found Sharifah washing the utensils.

"I told you to stop doing such work. Where are the others? I said all of them must wake up early every day and do some housework. They think they will just eat and sleep," she shouted as she continued to our room.

"Look at all of them – all sleeping like dogs. I wonder what you people will become in the future. You are always thinking about sleeping and about no other thing. Sharifah . . ." she called out.

"Yes aunt" Sharifah replied.

"Please bring me a glass of water."

She poured the water in all my siblings' ears. They suddenly woke up and looked at her like cats on hot bricks.

"Good morning, aunt," they wobbled.

"Didn't I tell you all to wake up and start doing some house chores? What are you still waiting for to wake up," She hollered.

Wanyana immediately led Nansubuga and Mpagi to the kitchen and told them to finish washing the utensils. She later came and joined me. The clothes were too many and dirty. After washing, we went to the dining room to take some tea. Before we could finish up the breakfast, there was our aunt with the next job, "hurry up and clean the house. You are the ones who always make it dirty."

We finished up the breakfast and started mopping the house. I cleaned the sitting room and the dining room, Wanyana cleaned aunt's bedroom and Esther's, Nansubuga cleaned Ernest's while Mpagi tidied Elijah's bedroom. After cleaning the main house, we went to the boys' quarter and mopped everywhere. We were extremely tired after cleaning the house, so we decided to rest a bit. As soon as our heads touched the pillow, we were out like a light.

We were only woken up by Sharifah at around 1:30 pm to take lunch. By the time we woke up, Esther, Elijah and Ernest had all come back from school. We sat at the dining table and enjoyed the delicious matoke and fresh fish meal.

"I think you know what to do next?" Aunt asked after ensuring that everyone had finished eating his/her food.

"Mummy, you know what I am going to do next? Sleep sweet sleeping. Tomorrow is a school day. Not so mummy?" Esther said.

"Yes my, dear . . . I guess Elijah and Ernest should follow suit. Tomorrow is school day and so you have to rest now and wake up and do your homework," she said as she pointed at Esther.

Esther, Elijah and Ernest suddenly rose up to go to their beds.

"Nansubuga and Mpagi, you are washing the utensils, Sharifah will prepare supper, as Wanyana and Masembe iron the clothes. I hope I have made myself clear," she said as she went to her bed.

Before we could finish up ironing, she woke up and came to where we were, "Look!! You did not wash my skirt properly," she said as she took a close look at her skirt. "See the stains in it. No wonder all your clothes are filthy and tarnished . . . If you cannot wash my clothes properly, tell me. I will wash them myself. You think I do not know how to wash them?"

She quickly commanded Wanyana to go and re-wash it and continued checking the remaining clothes.

"I do not really understand you people. Check the way you are ironing your uncle's shirt. It is as if you do not want to do what you have been asked to do," she told me.

After supper that very night, as uncle and aunt were making for their bedroom, she said, "Masembe, please help me and clean this dining room properly. It cannot stay in dirty state."

I mopped the floor as my siblings tidied up the dining table and the sitting room. Before we finished, she came back and told us to make sure that the kitchen was also clean before we slept.

Aunt became so boorish to us. She used to stay at home the whole day and she required us to do all the house chores under strict instructions. We would always be the last people to sleep and the first to wake up.

While my uncle's children went to the expensive and good schools, I and my siblings remained at home. My uncle never bothered to take us to school once again. A lot had changed about him. He was not the caring and responsible uncle we used to stay with during those days in the village. He was always too busy to attend to us. He used to leave very early in the morning and would come back only at around 8.00pm.

One time as he was leaving the house for work, I ran up to him and said, "Uncle, we haven't yet started school."

He replied, "I don't have enough money to finance your education right now. The problem is that you are many, but I promise you will go to school as soon as I get enough money. It is just that business is not good these days. I hope you realize the level of inflation in the country. But don't worry, I will send all of you to school," he then recklessly drove off.

The next day, I decided to go back to the institute, where I had never returned since my mother's death. I pleaded with my uncle as he was going to work and he decided to drop me there. I reached and went straight to class. I thought my uncle would feel mortified and he would at one moment decide to pay my fees. However, it wasn't the case.

One day, he gave me fifty thousand Ugandan shillings to pay part of my fees. When Aunt saw what had happened, she opposed it.

"Darling, you know we have not yet paid Esther's fees but you are here giving the money to Mase. I think he could have waited till we collect more money," she said as she tried to remove the money from my hands.

"No! Leave that money with him. I will bring some money to pay for Esther's fees in the evening when I get back," he replied and quickly left.

That was the last time I received money from uncle. As time went by, school fees became a burden to me. Regrettably, the biting poverty and the fact that I was always on the list of school fees defaulters made me drop out of school. This was the hardest decision I had ever made, but life gave me no other options.

Time passed and uncle started realizing the ruthless and hard-nosed way in which aunt treated us.

They would also get into quarrels and fist fights because of the way uncle backed us.

"Look at the way they have muddled the dining room. I am tired of cleaning it every time they finish eating from it. They will never sit here anymore," aunt told uncle.

The next day as we had gathered on the dining table to take lunch, she asked Sharifah where she had put the only mat that they owned.

"It is in my room," Sharifah replied.

"Please go and bring it," aunt ordered.

Sharifah left and quickly came back with a mat.

"From today onwards, the three of you, Seguya, Nansubuga and Mpagi should never sit on my chairs again, because you keep on disorganizing them. You should always sit on this mat," she said as she tried to lay down the mat.

"Put it back. Do you want to destroy it too?" she bellowed at Nansubuga after seeing that she was playing with Esther's doll. "I do not ever want to see any of you playing with any of my children's toys here. First of all, you do not know how to play with them and secondly, you are so destructive. I am very certain you will break off the head within a minute."

She never wanted her children to play with any of my little brothers and sisters. She always said they were illiterates and weren't her children's type. I came to realize that her beauty was only skin-deep. I started hating her so much.

One night she said to Mpagi. "No wonder you are as stupid as your parents. They were so irresponsible. That's why they died before waiting for you all to grow up. I told you never to sit in my chairs again, but you are perverse."

I'm not sure what could have possibly spurred her to make such a statement. It hit me so hard; I just couldn't believe what I had just heard. After hearing it, I went straight to my bed. The night was so long and my companion was my tear-stained pillow. I just couldn't stop crying.

A few days after this incident, life turned so lonely. Those turned out to be the most trying moments in my life. Day by day life was becoming so unendurable. I realized that a woman who we thought would be the best aunt in the world had turned into a Beelzebub. One day she even threatened to throw us out of the house.

"Are you deaf? I do not understand why you cannot understand whatever I tell you. I remember telling you not to play with my children's' toys. You are about to leave my house. I am so tired of telling old people who cannot listen," she shouted in rage.

Since we were shunned by family and people who were claiming to be our friends, I realized that it was time for me to face the world's challenges and look after my siblings. Life seemed so unbearable; it was just hell on earth. I could hardly comprehend what was going on around me. It was as if we were being punished for a crime we never committed.

My aunt always complained that we were the reason why they were being strained on feeding. As a way of supplementing the home budget, I decided to go and look out for a job.

As a desperate orphan with very miserable experiences and burdened with the deep struggle to make both ends meet, I headed to the streets in search of work. I moved to a number of places, in the rain and sun, during day and night. I trotted places, until I found my lucky day. That day is still vivid in my memory.

As I was walking on the streets of Kampala one day, I came across a signpost of a Non Governmental Organization called "Voiceless Orphans." I stood there, thought for a minute, gathered all the confidence and then encouraged myself to knock on the blue gate. A very tall dark-skinned gateman, commonly known as an askari in Uganda, chirped with a vivid face from a very small rectangular window on the fence, stared at me, and then came out.

"Aaaahh yes . . . how are you?" he asked.

"I am fine. How are you sir?" I replied.

"So, who are you looking for?"

"I would like to see the receptionist."

He gave me a book to sign in and finally let me in.

"Go in, turn to your right and enter through a very big glass door. That is where the reception is."

"Thank you so much, sir"

I went to where he exactly directed me. I saw large-figured portraits of orphans on the walls, a woolen gray carpet on the floor and very nice furniture. There was a big bouquet of multi-coloured flowers on the reception's desk. There was a small boy aged fifteen or so who looked so nice and alluring.

"Good morning, sir," he greeted me.

"Good morning. I wanted to know if you had some jobs here," I said.

"I am not so sure . . . but allow me to go and inquire from the human resource manager's office. Take a seat there, and I will come shortly. "

I sat down on the chairs waiting with all kinds of fear and qualms troubling my mind. It was a strange sensation for me to feel so alone in the world. After a few minutes, the little boy came back.

"There are no more jobs here, but the Executive Director has said you can see him in his office. Turn on to your left, climb those steps and reach the next floor. Enter in the 3rd office on your right," he said.

Fear gripped me as I reached the Executive Director's office. I first faltered to enter, but I realized it would be so bad for me if I just left. I encouraged myself and I finally knocked on the door. I was welcomed in and was offered a seat. There was a nice-looking man with a nice smile and a very deep voice.

"I was told you wanted a job," he said.

"Yes, sir," I replied.

"We do not have jobs right now, but we want some volunteers. A volunteer is expected to have studied up to Advanced level and must be tender to children. We would like a person with very good communication skills both verbally and Para linguistically. He must know how to speak English so fluently, since most of the sponsors in this organization understand and speak mostly English. He/she is also expected to be so hardworking and willing to work as an individual and as a team with little or no supervision. You can leave your application, C.V and academic credentials if you are eligible and like the offer."

"Yes, sir, I want it."

"A volunteer like you will not be paid a monthly salary, but you will be entitled to weekly allowances of thirty thousand shillings and are required to work from Monday to Friday, 8:00 am to 5:00 pm. Saturdays are not compulsory. You may or may not come. You can now go."

I stood up with a lot of incredulity. He looked at me, and later called me back.

"Yes, sir," I said.

"Can you tell me a little about yourself?"

"I am an orphan and I was born in the year 1982. I finished my primary and secondary education and later dropped out after joining an institute due to fees problems. Before mother died, she used to teach us how to weave baskets and take them to the market and that is how we used to earn a living. I also . . ."

"You mean you can weave baskets very well?"

"Yes sir."

"Come back after two days with all your credentials and start work."

"Thank you so much, sir"

I stood up and quickly left his office. As I reached the reception's desk, the little boy just sensed that everything had gone on well, and congratulated me.

That was the day I was given a chance to work with my heart. It wasn't only my heart that was involved but rather the will to make it a turning point in our life. When I was asked to join Voiceless Orphans, I was thrilled and just couldn't wait to start work.

I went back home, and everyone could easily notice the smiles on my face. Sharifah asked me what had happened, but I refused to tell her the good news. After supper, we went to our room and Wanyana led us through the prayers. Just after the prayers, I broke the ice and everyone was too happy for me. I told them not to tell anyone about the conditions or the little money I was going to be earning.

Prickle in a Dream

On the day I was required to report to work, I got to work so early and ready to both learn and work. I again saw the pleasant face of that sweet little orphan who welcomed me. He was so sweet and friendly, and he turned out to be a darling among them all. Slowly over time I learnt to love all the children equally. Every one of them had a story to tell. Their stories were so touching and inspiring, and were stories of hope and determination. I felt so uplifted and encouraged.

I learnt a lot and it gave me the urge to work so hard. I could see the children in the orphanage and could get encouraged a lot. They cared for and loved each other so much. I could look at their happy faces and could also smile inside my heart.

"Uncle, I want to play football with you," Dan, a little boy of around 5 would tell me. He loved football very much and would enjoy playing it with me.

"Uncle, I want you to teach me science. I want to become a doctor so that I can earn a lot of money." Sharon of 7 years once told me.

Once in a while, we would be called to talk to the children. One day an orphaned conference entitled "There is hope for an orphaned child," was organized and I was given a chance to make a speech on this occasion. I was nervous and excited at the same time. I gave it a go and this is what I went on to say at the conference:

"I think there is so much in life than just having a family and friends. If you are unfortunate and have grown up without parents, that is not the end of the world. Just hold on and put your focus onto that dream. It hurts knowing that you have nobody to

depend on, but still you have your own future to look unto, and forget about what the past had in stock for you. Your name is inscribed in the palms of God's hands. He knows the cries of your heart and loves you so much.

He sees the tears that you cry and hears your voice whenever you call unto him. Whenever you are feeling alone and everyone else is against you, remember that God is for you. His love for you never fluctuates. Put your faith in the hands of the potter-God. Remember, you are not just a face in the crowd; you are the disciple Jesus keeps on loving. He promised never to leave nor forsake you. What all of you here have got to know is that your beauty can only be recognized if you are sincere to others, if you love the unloved and if you care for those in need, not as you look, walk or wear. Love one another as Christ loves you. May God richly bless you all."

After I had finished, people clapped their hands. I felt so happy that they appreciated what I had said to them. I felt so motivated and treasured. Children started coming to me for guidance, thinking I was an expert in counseling and guidance. None of them ever thought that I was also an orphan like them. I would always give them motivating Bible verses and real life stories of people. I loved all the moments I spent in the organization.

One of the organization's projects was doing crafts with the children. Since I had gained some skills from my mother, I was requested to teach the children crafts. I worked so hard since I knew that this was my "bread and butter." After gaining more skills, I realized that one can make money from this kind of work.

With the little money that I had saved, I decided to try my luck on being a craftsman. Fortunately I was well-trained in making necklaces and bracelets. I was determined to take on this untapped gift.

I went to the craft market and bought a few materials and then headed to uncle's home ready to start on this new world of adventure. At first it wasn't easy because making them was one thing and having them bought was another. The biggest challenge was that I had no experience in the marketing and selling of the jewelry.

After making the jewelry, I set off to the streets of Kampala in search for a market. The city was so big, making it hard for me to find my way through it all alone. All the places I looked at seemed so similar. Each time I moved, I found myself coming back to the same spot I was in before. What made it worse was the city council law enforcement. Since I was shabbily dressed, I was misunderstood for a petty thief or conman. The people I met referred to me as a muyaaye, which can be translated as a thief or lumpen.

Since I had no license permitting me to do sale on the city streets, I got into trouble with the city council officers; it took me a very long time to convince them about my plight.

"Show me your trading license," one officer asked me.

"Sir, I do not have a trading license. I started up this business after life had proved to be so bad for me and my siblings. We are orphans and we do not have anyone to take care of us. Please allow me to continue with my business," I pleaded.

"No, do not leave him. He should produce his license now or else we confiscate his goods," another officer said.

"By the way, look at his necklaces. I think my wife will love this one," another one said as he checked through all my necklaces.

"Please, do not take my things. I only want to take my siblings to school. Life is not good for us. Every other person abandoned us. Please let me do this business," I pleaded again.

"Okay . . . but the next time we come back here, you must be having a trading license. Clear?" another one finally felt pity for me and they all left me to work.

"Very clear, sir," I replied.

During the first couple of days on the streets, I hardly got a customer for the bracelets and necklaces. Since I wasn't ready to fail, I went to Kisekka market.

This market dealt mostly in both new and old vehicle spare parts. It had about 5,000 official traders and hundreds of other people doing vehicle repairs. I confidently entered the market and asked some woman who was seated on her stall having lunch if she could be interested in the bracelets and necklaces I had.

"No . . . I don't like. I do not think your products are good and original. I think they are the fake things I always buy from this market," one woman in the market said.

"Bring and I shall take a look," another woman on the neighboring stall said.

I gave her my bracelets and necklaces and she looked at them. She saw how nice they were and started taking them around most women in the market. She liked them and that was the day I made my first sale. This was more than a miracle because I sold up everything I had to her. I even got more orders from different women. I was so excited about this, not knowing that the many orders I was receiving were due to the fact that my jewelry was beautiful and cheap. Now I realize that I was being cheated.

The woman who seemed to have come to my rescue and bought my jewelry gave me half the actual price of what the jewelry was going for in the market. At that time I didn't know about all this, and since my main concern was to make sales, I thanked this lady thousands of times for buying off my jewelry.

Whenever city council officers came to the market to check for the licenses, people who didn't have licenses would always be running around and hiding themselves in all the possible safe places and would only come back to sell their goods after realizing that they had left. That was how I used to survive in the market. Whenever I would hear of people running, I would collect my goods and equipment and would hide in the safest place around.

Though the money I used to get was chicken feed, I slowly made gains and started saving some little money. I discovered that it was a lucrative deal for me since many people came to like my goods.

When my aunt saw this, she made life harder for us than before. She could even deny us food, saying that I was working.

"Since you are a man now and you are earning a lot of money, no more food for you in the house," she would say.

It came to a time when even the children started telling us to leave their parents' home. One time I overheard Esther telling Nansubuga. "Why don't you go back to your home? You are not part of our family. First of all, you are not educated and secondly, you look so malnourished. You do not even know good English."

I knew that this was the work of the devil, and that all this was an influence from their mother who surely wanted us out of their home.

One time my aunt found Nansubuga with the TV remote.

"What are you doing with my remote? Do you want to spoil it the second time? Do you know how to even use it? Did you have TVs at your home? Put it down before I come near you! Stupid girl," she shouted at her.

I heard this and I felt so small. Of course we had never watched a TV in the whole of our lives, but was it a crime?

I used to think that poverty was only being hungry, naked and homeless, but I later learnt that the poverty of being unwanted, unloved and uncared for is the greatest poverty. I came to hate this kind of poverty with all my heart.

Chapter 5

A GREAT TREK TO INDEPENDENCE

One day when I returned from work, I found my disabled brother seated on the ground in the hot scorching sun with marks of dry tears down his gaunt chin. Beads of sweat were profusely streaking down his face which showed that he had been seated there for a longer time. He had bruises on his arms where he had been whipped with a belt.

After making inquiries, I learnt that Seguya was serving a punishment for eating something from the neighbors. That morning, my aunt and her children ate up all the breakfast leaving nothing for my siblings. Seguya was so hungry that he decided to go to the neighborhood to seek something for the stomach. On reaching there, he was offered some bananas. Since this poor little boy was so hungry, he accepted the bananas with open arms, but he did he know that aunt was watching from a distance.

"It was not long before aunt surfaced. She came where he was, picked him up and headed home. On reaching home, she slapped and hit him several times while abusing and cursing him. She made a particular statement which was so hurting. She said that we were all ungrateful and suggested that if we wanted good things, we should go and ask our parents to rise from their graves and come and provide for us. She also said that we were so stupid just like our parents. She added that we should never dare interact with her children, lest we could infect them with our ungratefulness." Nansubuga reported to me.

These words were so strong and harsh. They kept on ringing in my mind. I wept all night and hardly got a wink of sleep. I asked God all sorts of questions.

At one point, I cursed the day I was born and wished I could die and go meet my mother in the life of the dead. This was so painful, much more painful than the day I said farewell to my mother.

The next day, I made up my mind to stand up and defend my siblings; I went and confronted my aunt. I had a big argument with her. That, however, did not solve anything. She called me nasty names and I refused to just sit there and listen to it. I said something to her and she just took a shot at me. I ended up crying and going to our room. A minute or so later she came to our door and knocked. I did not want to even see her face at that point. Since I never had a lock on the door, she just opened it and kept talking down to me.

Even after she was gone, I continued howling uncontrollably. I was so befuddled and not sure what I could do next. I tried to turn to my God since He is the food to a man with an empty stomach, but all I could say was "God, why us?" It seemed as though God was so far away. I even thought that He was not seeing the tears that I kept on shedding.

As the morning drew nearer, something came into my mind. I decided that enough was enough. If I did nothing, it could be like a ghost tying my hands and shutting my mouth and not letting me live up to my responsibility of taking care of my siblings. I knew that it was only my efforts that could brighten and bring smiles to my brothers and sisters.

It was time to step out of this cruel nest and find one of our own. I woke up very early in the morning and instead of heading to work, I went house hunting. I had decided that enough was enough and that the only island of escape was to step out of this nest and create a nest of our own. With the savings that I had made, I went in search for a house.

I went from one place to another until I came to a particular place in the slums of Mengo Kisenyi – a suburb of Kampala. I settled for one particular place there. It was not the best place to live in and worse still to raise my siblings, but I was so determined to move on.

In my first scrutiny of the house, the outer appearance gave me a brief glance of the rooms. The walls around were wearing out and there seemed no sign of having them renovated. I was however impressed that although the rooms were crowded, the walls around could provide some bit of security.

The place had dilapidated rooms featuring small thin and weak wood windows and doors. The blue paint had turned into creamish. The bathrooms were not any better. When I inquired from the landlord whether the room could have some paint uplift he looked at me and smiled.

He said, "Son, I understand the shape this house is in, but remember you are just a tenant. Tenants never own houses. You wait until you build your own home so that you can enjoy the luxuries of a good and beautiful home."

The fact that the market was only a 5 minute walk away from this place enticed me to it and I ended up paying for it. It is this place I call home, sweet home, even today. The environment around is not favorable but still it is home, sweet home. At least here we are no longer harshly treated by relatives. Gone are the inglorious days when we used to be treated like abandoned luggage.

When I returned home that evening, I broke the good news to all my siblings when we were in our room. "I have gotten a house in which we are going to start a new life from. Pack all our chattels. We shall leave tomorrow morning."

They delightfully packed whatever belonged to us. They were so glad that we were soon leaving the rich but unloving people.

All the mistakes committed by one person who was supposed to be an instrument of direction did finally go away. This was not a time of looking back, but a time of moving on. Life gave us no options but rather accept the fact that life is not about leaning on one person, but rather making something out of what you want your life to be.

The following sunny morning in the month of March, I broke the news to my uncle in the morning as he was leaving home for work.

"Uncle, I got a house in which I and my siblings will be staying in. We have finished packing our possessions and shall be leaving today evening. Thank you so much for the help and love you have always shown us. May God richly bless you."

"Mase, whatever has made you leave that soon? I hope everything is okay?" he asked.

"Yes uncle. We do not have any problem. We are all fine. I just wanted us to start another life of being independent," I said.

"Okay, but make sure you always stay in touch."

He drove off and went to work. We boarded a taxi from his home to the new taxi park until we set foot in our new home. This marked the beginning of our autonomy.

Fatigue plunged me like a sharp knife. We said our prayers and went to bed. When I lay on the bed that night, all I could remember was being awoken by sunlight that was gleaming through the tiny window. I guess I must have gone through a dozen of sleep cycles.

I knew supporting the family single handily was not going to be easy. Everything seemed not right. I imagined so many things. The fact that everyone had dropped out of school made it even so difficult for me. With computerization and advancement in the world I knew that since we were all drop outs, we were headed to doom and that the future was dark. During all this time I kept the faith going and always prayed to God to open doors for me and my siblings.

The next morning as I woke up to bathe, a short, dark-skinned man sitting next to the bathroom door said, "your money?"

I looked at him with a puzzled face, "Pardon, Sir!" I confusingly said.

"I asking, where your money . . . me money?" he shouted angrily.

"Money? For what sir?" I asked.

"Money for what?" he snarled, "Musajja, look, this Kampala . . . everything money . . . money . . . Bathroom . . . toilet . . . water . . . and food. Simanyi, you village come? I know you people from village, everything free, free. Here no free. Pay 200 and you water bathe," he shouted.

This man dropped a bombshell when he told me that we had to pay 200 every time we used the toilets and another 200 for the bathrooms. Since I never had the 200 that day, I went back into the house, dressed up and quickly left for work.

"Mase, can you imagine that man near the toilets asked us for money to use the toilets and the bathroom?" Wanyana reported to me when I came back from work.

"Yes! I forgot to let you know. He even refused to let me bathe in the morning. He wanted his money. I think I should go and inquire from the land lord," I answered him.

When I went to the landlord, he also said the same thing.

"But sir, look, we are five people staying in this house. You cannot be expecting everyone here to pay two hundred whenever we use these facilities," I besought his sympathy.

"Ha ha ha, you never cease to amaze me. So how much did you want to pay?" he angrily smiled.

"Allow all of us to pay five hundred shillings for the whole day for both the toilets and the bathroom," I humbly pleaded.

He replied, "What are you saying? Which mathematics have you used to come up with that figure? Young boy, each one of you has to pay two hundred shillings to use the services. No negotiation!" he said assertively.

I slowly walked away from him and went to break the bad news to my dear siblings.

"Mase, has he allowed? What has he said?" Wanyana anxiously asked.

"He has refused whatever I have told him." I replied.

"So how are we really going to manage? Imagine I visit the toilet 6 times a day, you 3 times a day, Mpagi four times a day, Nansubuga may be one time, and Seguya twice, and on top of that we all have to bathe. Mase, we can't pay all that money. We can use it to feed us for a whole week," Wanyana said.

"I have a plan you people," Nansubuga happily spoke out. "Why don't we get buckets? Yes five buckets? Ummmh, we are five people. We give everyone his own bucket. He/she uses it for the whole day, and then we take them there at once at night. It works, doesn't it?"

"Yes," Mpagi interrupted, "Nansubuga is right. That is the reason why I love you. In fact, all of us should use the same bucket for the whole day so that instead of spending two thousand shillings for only the toilet, we shall spend only two hundred and for the bathroom, I think all of us will be bathing from the house."

All my siblings supported the idea and that was exactly what we did. What a beautiful idea of saving! Life has surely moved on smoothly since then.

While in the new house, we encountered many challenges. Times came when we could go away with only a single meal which was mainly of cereals. I seemed not to save anything. Money always burnt a hole in my pocket.

In front of our house, there was a small corridor which could lead one to Namirembe road. Many women dressed in skimpy clothes and their men always ogled as they used that corridor to reach their favorite meeting points. The place was always noisy especially on Friday

Prickle in a Dream

and Saturday nights. Loud music blared from all corners of the thriving nightclubs and discotheques around the place. Saturday merriment always started earlier at around 5 pm and would end after midnight. You could hear drunkards shout on top of their voices as they sang along the songs that were always being played. One could even hear some people laughing endlessly as they watched the so-called karaoke on Wednesdays. During football match broadcast, I could see people standing in endless queues as they entered the gates of Nakivubo stadium. Football fans always passed through our small corridor with their faces painted with the colours of their favorite teams. They would pass around the place with their "vuvuzelas" in their hands shouting the names of their best players and betting about the goals they were going to score.

Unlike a boy of my age who spends his money on having fun with their peers, dating girls and parting endlessly, mine was spent chasing the almighty dollar, in order to fend for my little siblings. I was even so lucky that despite the environment that we stayed in, none of my siblings ever wished to step a foot out of the house to go and "enjoy" life.

I always consoled myself with the Bible verse in Matthew 6.26: *Look at the birds of the air: they neither sow nor reap nor gather into barns, and yet your heavenly Father feeds them. Are you not of more value than they?*

Each time I felt low, I could recite this verse and get the determination to face another tomorrow.

Later on, a friend of mine in the same business introduced me to other bigger and busier markets such as Owino and Nakasero to increase my sales. All my siblings had become experts in making jewelry, so they would stay at home busy, making what was to be sold the next day.

Owino, commonly known as down town, was the busiest of all markets in Kampala and it sprawled around the Nakivuubo Stadium, near the taxi parks. This market, like other markets, was a long sea of stalls selling cheap clothes, food, spices and household goods such as home made irons, but it was most popular with travelers for its wide range of second-hand clothes from Europe, Asia and the USA. All prices for different goods were negotiable and they started from cheap to getting cheapest with bargaining. We used to raise our prices whenever we could see a mzungu (white person) sniffing around. The place used to crowd a lot especially on holidays and on weekends, as nymphets rummaged around for new stocks for party wear, dinner dresses, shoes and jewelry.

Nakasero market was a lot more pleasant but smaller than Owino. It was located below Kampala Road and better suited for a relaxed saunter. This market was divided into two areas, one located in a gorgeous but old building and another located in partially covered vicinity. Traders in the building dealt mostly in hardware, clothes and jewelry, while those in the partially covered vicinity dealt especially in fruits and vegetables.

Shortly, I stopped trading in Nakasero because the market was too far away from home and I always got less sales there compared to what I was sure to get in Owino and Kisekka markets.

One Sunday afternoon, when my sister Wanyana came from church, she came home with a business contact card of a British citizen by the name of Mr. Mathew. She entered the house as she held her Bible tightly on her chest and she was wearing a very cheerful face. She suddenly removed the Bible, flipped several pages until she picked out a small light coloured hard piece of paper. As she was happily handing it over to me, Nansubuga and Mpagi battled for it. Nansubuga suddenly drew her hands away from it. Mpagi looked at him, turned it upside down, and then handed it over to Wanyana who later passed it to me.

"Mase, see, I got this," she merrily said.

"Where have you got it from?" I said as I took a close look on the card. It had his full names, his company name, and his post in the company, his email address and his telephone contacts.

"Look! He is the managing Director of a company in the United Kingdom."

"Today I sat next to this white man in church. Before the service commenced, we greeted each other. After service I was walking home when this gentleman called me. I straight away recognized him as the person I was sitting next to in church. He then asked me for directions. That was where I got to talk to him at length. He told me that he had come to Uganda on research. He then asked me if I were in school. I told him all about myself. He felt so touched and gave me his business card. He told me to contact him any time from that day. He also said that he would have visited us, but he had to go and catch the next flight at around 4pm to Britain. He told me that he had spent two weeks in Uganda and he enjoyed his time here. He said that he was willing to help me with my education," Wanyana narrated.

It was joy in the house; this news was a ray of sunshine in my day. Nansubuga, Seguya and Mpagi all shouted so loudly in excitement of the good news.

"We are going to Britain. I am going to start speaking fluent English," Nansubuga shouted out as she danced around the house.

The fact that we had stayed in far-flung villages the whole of our lives made it impossible for any of us to understand what an email address meant, or what its use was. We could not call him since the cost of making a call to Britain was really too high.

After making so many inquiries for several weeks, I was told that an email was internet-based and I, therefore, had to go to a nearby internet café, open an email address, and then be able to send him an email. I was directed to click-now internet café on park view hotel near the old taxi park.

"Good morning madam!" I greeted the lady seated on the counter, "I was directed here and I would like to send an email to someone in Britain. He is called . . ."

"Yes, you can. You do not have to tell me all the details of the person you are sending it to since this is a public area where everyone's ear is wide open to hear what you are telling me," she humbly interrupted.

"So do you have an email address?" she continued.

"No . . . No, actually, I want you to open one for me now. How much will it cost me?" I asked.

"Only two thousand shillings," she answered.

Although this sounded a lot to my ears, I accepted since I really wanted to contact Mr. Matthew. I knew he was going to be a savior to our family.

"Okay madam," I replied.

She helped me open up an email address. After opening it, she asked for two thousand shillings more to help me send an email. I checked in my pockets and there was no more money left.

"Madam, I do not have enough money right now, but please do not close my email. I will come back tomorrow with the money and you help me send," I calmly said.

"No! I cannot close it. It is the website that can close your email address if you take long to use it. The problem is I may not work tomorrow so let me just show you what to do so that you go back home, write all your words on a piece of paper, go to any other internet café and send your email." She replied as she showed me how to send an email step by step.

I requested her for a piece of paper and wrote each step she told me. I just wrote whatever she told me though I was not so sure of most of the words she used like, Mozilla Firefox, website, Google, etc.

I happily went back home and promised Wanyana that we were going to contact Mr. Matthew. She became very ecstatic as I told her the good news.

A couple of days later, I and Wanyana went into an internet café, got into my email address and sent him a message. It was to Mr. Mathew whom we later referred to as Daddy.

One day when we least expected to hear from him, we got an email from him, printed it out and took it home.

It read,

Hello Wanyana,

How are you? I hope everything is fine with you and your family. I am very sorry I have taken long to reply because I have been so busy and could hardly get any time to reply you. I felt so happy reading from you.

I reached safely and I was so happy to see my wife and children once again. They have all sent their lovely greetings to you.

I thank the Lord so much and I am happy to tell you that from today, I will be taking care of your tuition and all basic needs. Whatever you need, do not hesitate to contact me any time.

I pray God protects you and keep you safe. Be a good girl and always put your trust in God.

NB: send me personal details as soon as you receive this message

Regards
Matthew

Once again, we were keyed up over Mr. Matthew's email and continued to pray about it. After reading this email again and again in disbelief, the following afternoon we went back to the café and sent Mr Mattew Wanyana's details.

Not long after he sent in money that we used to pay for Wanyana's tuition. This was really a blessing because this money was more than enough for Wanyana alone. We used it to cater for other needs too. He and his wife continuously called us to find out how we were and to encourage us. He would also send us packages containing clothes, shoes, sweets and biscuits. This was surely God's gifts and I continued to have faith in God for all the good works he was doing for us.

With the help of Mr. Mathew's funding and the little money I was saving, Mpagi and Nansubuga were able to go to school too. I managed to also purchase two small wooden beds and three mattresses that we were able to share whenever we needed to sleep.

I could stay at home with Seguya making crafts as the rest went to school. I fell short on having to take Seguya to school because all the schools for disabled children like him were too expensive. I, however, tried to teach him a few things while at home. He is a bright young boy full of happiness; I thank the Lord for him each day.

These happy days came to a halt though. One day Mr. Matthew's wife called us and informed us that Mr. Matthew had died. His death only added acid to the flames. We could hardly digest the deplorable news. This news caused a big blow to us all; he had become a daddy to us all and I had started seeing the bright side of life.

This news came along with many trying and challenging times. We felt so abandoned and forgotten once again. I would call his mobile number many times, and the only response I received was that the number was off. I tried pleading with his wife to help us push on, but she said that she was also a "stay-home" mother/wife who never had a job, and her children were also still young.

Wanyana cried her eyes out, and made it even harder for me to concentrate since I was so worried about the outcomes of her sorrowful state.

Once again, due our inability to pay university fees, Wanyana and Mpagi dropped out of University, making it the second time to drop out of school. I was only able to continue paying tuition for Nansubuga since it was the only thing I could fix in the tight budget we had at home. We were forced to get along on a shoestring. Life had become so difficult for us again.

I have always remembered what Mr. Mathew said to us one day before he died. He said, "Always avoid envying those who have money so that you can emulate them and benefit from their experiences and help. This is one thing that has always been encouraging me to work hard for the betterment of my siblings."

I also recalled that at one time my mother told me: "It's true that wealth is a source of trouble and restlessness but in life if you want to succeed you should avoid people who are selfish and do not care about others. At one time when you ever decide to start hunting for money, ease the burden of dishonesty because all things will require some degree of honesty since if people prove that you are dishonest they shun you."

Prickle in a Dream

While making crafts one day, I felt disappointed by a neighbor's child who tampered with my finished bracelets; he had ruined a week's work. This was like the disappearance of the most awaited fortune. It was then that I asked Wanyana to start helping me with making the jewelry. I knew with hard work and determination as a family, we could make it. I decided to teach everyone this craft work, because I knew it could be of help to everyone at home.

The sales were not as good as they were a couple of years back. Many people had joined the same business and therefore there were limited customers unlike before. God has, however, been faithful amidst the suffering. He has provided for our day to day living.

One day I went to work. The day turned out to be so bad that I hardly got any customer, however much I ran after them. I tried beguiling them with my beautiful voice by composing advertising songs for my jewelry but it was all in vain. I was so disappointed and saddened that I decided to go back home.

As I continued moving so despondently, I stepped on something. I quickly looked down to see what it was – it was a small but nice-looking leather money purse. I swiftly picked it up and realized it was made from original leather material. I knew it had been dropped by someone very rich and well off. I looked around for anyone who could be the owner of this elegant purse but all the people I saw did not fit its ownership. I then opened it. There was a golden chain, a bunch of keys, three Fifty thousand shillings notes, some few coins, an ATM card issued by one of the big banks in the country and a business card. I panicked a lot after setting my eyes on all those things.

From the little English I had learnt, I could clearly read the words that were written on the business card in the beautiful purse. I knew that it was of a classy person. I walked home, wondering what I could do with all the money that was in the purse.

"Mase, can't you see that God has just blessed you with this money? First of all, you have not got any money from work, and there will not be any food to feed on tomorrow. Nansubuga has not yet completed her school fess. Take that money and use it to buy food and also to complete Nansubuga's fees," my inner voice told me.

Remembering mother's words of wisdom, I knew that it would be very bad if I removed even a single coin from it. Mother had always stressed that I had to work hard to earn every single penny. Being a Christian, I could remember a verse that encouraged hard work and that man shall eat from the result of his sweat. So I could not remove anything from it.

"This is too much money for me. What if robbers have seen me picking it and they come and break into our house during the night? No . . . no, I will not take it home. Let me take it back to where I have got it from," I thought to myself.

As I changed the direction to go back to where I had picked the money purse from, I suddenly stopped and stood still. "May be I should call this number . . . but

Prickle in a Dream

I do not have a phone and these public phones on the streets are now closed," I thought aloud.

"Mase, take it home. You will take it to the owner tomorrow," I told myself. All of a sudden, I looked on my right and my left and immediately ran off, and only stopped when I had reached our house door. I thumped the door until Mpagi came and opened for me. They all looked at my startled face and guessed something was wrong. I suddenly sat down and showed them the purse. Wanyana opened it first and threw it down in shock.

"Mase . . . where have you got it from?" she asked as my other siblings battled over who would check it first.

"I picked it as I was coming from work," I explained, "but I am so confused of what to do next."

"Just do what is right, no matter the cost. God who sees even in darkness will reward you. Mase, we may be poor, but that does not give us the right to take what does not belong to us . . ." Wanyana said.

"What if it is God who has given it to us? Haven't you seen what he has gone through the whole day? He left work so disenchanted today; he did not make any sales, and I am very sure we do not have anything to eat tomorrow," Mpagi interrupted.

"We badly need this money. Remember Nansubuga has not yet completed her school fees . . . plus the rent. The month is ending in two days' time and the landlord will be at our door knocking. And I hope you know this old man. He is always knocking at our door on every 1st of the month to collect his money," added Mpagi.

"Nansubuga, you have been so quiet, what is your opinion here?" I asked.

She replied, "I am so confused here. I know we really need this money . . . school fees, food, rent, sugar, soap and so on. But if surely God wanted us to have this money today, don't you think we would have received it without just picking a purse? . . . But then, why would such an incident just happen to us now that we do not even have a single coin in the house?"

"No, we cannot take this money that we have not worked for. I do not think God works in such ways. We may take this money and it just expands the problems we are already having. If it was intended for us, God would have found a better way of bringing it in our hands, not just through picking. So Mase, I suggest, you take the purse to the owner first thing tomorrow morning. If it was intended for us, it will indisputably be ours," Wanyana supplemented.

I listened to whatever they were saying and started thinking about all their suggestions and the reasons they were giving. I envisaged the situation we were going through. Definitely we needed this money. It was even going to be more than enough. I thought hard and long.

That night, I led the prayers before we slept and requested God to show us the truth and what to do next. I hid the money under my pillow and I slept. As I was still sleeping, I dreamt that mother was telling me to wake up very early in the morning to take the purse to the owner.

Prickle in a Dream

I woke up at the crack of dawn and prepared myself. I was very certain, according to the card that I was going to enter some important person's office, so I had to look well turned-out and presentable. I searched for my best wear, put it on and left the house. I wanted to reach the place as fast as I could since I had to come back and go to the market to sell my goods.

As I moved out of the house, I stood in the corridor for some few minutes, confused about the direction I was going to take. I was so mystified. I had never heard of Nkizi Road in the whole of my life. I decided to take the route which could lead me to Kampala Road. I moved very fast until I reached Hotel Equatorial. I stood there for some minutes until I saw some man stepping out of his car.

"Good morning, sir," I started.

"Good morning," he replied.

"I am looking for a company called Lulu constructors Limited on Nkizi Road," I said.

"I am sorry. I don't know it," he said as he quickly entered the Equatorial mall.

I continued padding along Kampala road until I found another man unlocking his saloon-car. I asked him if he knew where Lulu Constructors Limited was located.

"Yes, I know it very well, but it's too far from here. Do you know where Ben Kiwanuka Street is?" he asked.

"No sir." I replied.

"Actually, I was heading that side. May be I can take you and drop you there," he replied.

"Thank you so much, sir" I said. I quickly got into his car and he showed me the building on which the office was. As I walked in, I collided with a woman and all her documents fell on the ground. She was dressed in a corporate suit and high-heeled shoes. She must have been in her mid-thirties and I presumed she was a secretary in one of the offices on that building.

"I am very sorry, madam." I pleaded as I bent down to pick the documents that had fallen on the ground.

"No, no, please. You do not have to be sorry. It could have been my fault as well," she replied with a beaming smile on her face.

"Here, your envelope is here," I murmured.

"Oh, thank you so much. So where are you heading? Do you work around here?"

"No, I am actually looking for a company called…lulu . . ."

"Lulu?" she asked.

"Oh yes," I replied.

"You are almost there. Lulu is just opposite my office. Just go on the next floor and turn on your right. You will see their signpost on the 3rd door."

"Thank you so much, madam."

I had never seen a humble woman of her class. She must have been brought up in a good family. I was in awe. I wondered how such a smartly dressed lady would say sorry to a lousy peasant like me. Women of her class rarely associated with people like me. I was indeed astonished.

Following her directions, I was able to get to Lulu Constructions Limited. At the reception, there was a lady who asked me what I had come to do. I told her I wanted to see the managing director.

"Do you have an appointment with him?" he asked me.

"No, madam, but I was directed to him," I replied.

"He has gone for lunch. Take a seat there and wait for him," said the lady as she pointed to a free seat opposite the receptionist's desk. I stayed seated for about twenty minutes until a man of around 47, dressed in a black suit, a brown tie and black shoes, came in.

After he entered, the receptionist made a call to him and told him that someone wanted to see him. I was later directed to his office. I knocked and I was welcomed in. I looked at the wall and there hung a clock bearing the company's logo in its background. On his right was a table having a big flask, a bowl of sugar and three cups.

"Good morning, sir," I said to him.

"Good morning. How are you?" he replied.

"I am very fine, sir."

"So . . . what has brought you here?"

"As I was walking yesterday at around 7pm near Nakivubo Stadium, I stepped on a money purse. After opening it, I found your business card which had the directions to your company. Sir, I have come to bring it, here it is," I said as I pulled out the purse from my pocket.

He stretched out his hand to receive the purse and comfortably opened it as he swung in his chair.

"Wow….thank you so much. I do not know how I lost it. I reached home and I was not seeing this purse. I am mostly happy for my ATM. Can you believe I was in the process of acquiring another one? In fact let me first call this lady to inform her to stop the process," he said as he pulled out a Samsung phone from his chest pocket.

"Hello, Maria, do not bother getting for me another ATM. I have received the old one. Thank you," he put back the phone in his pocket.

"You mean the money is still in?" he surprisingly said, "no one can pick a purse and leave the money there. You are such an honest person."

He continued to check his money-purse, "you mean even the coins? You should have removed some money to cater for your transport. By the way where do you work from?" he asked.

"I work from Kiseka market," I replied.

"You mean you are one of these rich people dealing in motor vehicle spares?"

"No sir! I make jewelry from home, and then take it to either Kiseka or Owino markets to sell it."

"So how is the business?"

"It started well, but several people have joined the business and even customers have reduced. We hardly get enough money to feed on. What even . . ."

"Wait . . . you mean you are already married?"

"No, Sir, I stay and look after my younger siblings."

"It seems you are a very good person. I have actually been looking for a reliable person who can work for me as a messenger and I think your character suits the job. Are you willing to . . .?"

"Yes, sir . . . of course, sir . . . I am very hardworking and so reliable. I can even be cleaning your office every morning and . . ."

"No, don't worry, I already have a cleaner. You will be taking reports from my office to different clients."

"Thank you so much sir. I am very grateful to you. I appreciate the job you have given me and I promise to be a very good worker. And if there is anything else to do, sir, I am more than willing to take it up. So sir, when should I start?"

"Tomorrow, if it is okay for you?"

"Very okay sir. I will be here by 6:30 in the morning."

"No, that is too early. The office is usually opened at 8 am."

"Okay, sir. I will be here on time. Good bye, sir. Thank you once again."

"You are welcome. See you tomorrow."

I was too filled with sheer happiness. I walked out of the building bursting with joy. I could not believe I was going to start working in an office. I padded back home with this happy face.

"Haven't you gone to market today?" Seguya asked.

"I have got a very good job . . . and not just a job . . . but a job in an office. Can you imagine?"

"What? How? When?" Wanyana asked.

"The owner of the purse has given me a job in his office."

They all jumped up and down and shouted on top of their voices. They started composing new songs and dancing to the tune of them.

"My brother is working in an office? God, thank you so much. Jaja's blessings have worked . . . Mase; do you remember Jaja I used to help in the village? She blessed all of us and said we shall become prosperous. Now, I have started seeing that what she used to say was true." Nansubuga shouted.

"No more going to the market. At least now we have a better job," Mpanga said.

"No, that is not what we should do. We should continue making our jewelry and get some little money from there and supplement Mase's salary. Remember he is going to start earning a monthly salary which is always hard to manage, but if we have this other business, we can be getting what to feed on every day," Wanyana spoke out.

I woke up so early the next morning and headed to my workplace. My boss was a very good man and I enjoyed working for him. Though the kind of job I was doing was tiresome, I was always assured of a salary at the end of the month.

We continuously made our jewelry and Mpagi and Wanyana would take it to the markets for sale. They were not so experienced in marketing as I had become, but they learnt bit by bit. I could also help them on weekends, since I wasn't working on those days.

Through networking, we got in contact with the Hampton family in the United States of America. I later found out that this family was of Beth and Benny Hampton. As time went by I realized that Elizabeth Hampton (Beth) had so many mothering characteristics in her. She was not taken aback by colour or distance, she cared for us so much just like a mother could have cared and loved her children. She was a friend and comforter when I was facing trials, heavy and sudden, it was a time when adversity had taken the place of prosperity. It's then that I realized the reality of the saying that the dead are not dead. Although our parents are gone, they still live. This is evident in rebirth or the coming of the people we have come across. Along the way, I have been able to find love and guidance from people who have nurtured me and made me a strong person I am today.

After sharing my dream with Beth about Shalom, she got interested in my dream and accepted to stand with me in realizing this dream. Beth joined me in the dream as an ambassador and we were able to have Shalom For Africa registered in Texas USA.

I have faced so many challenges in life, perhaps too much for a twenty nine year old. I have come through many challenges like finding what my siblings will to eat, making sure that I pay up for the shelter we live in our clothing, and seeing that we are all healthy.

My success was not due to luck. It was blood, sweat and tears all the way. I am what I am because I have never stopped dreaming. I have always hoped for the things unseen.

Prickle in a Dream

I believe that there is so much in life than just having a family and friends. If you are unfortunate and have grown up without parents, that is not the end of the world. Just hold and put your focus onto that dream; you still have your own future though it hurts to think that you have nobody to depend on.

Yes, it is obvious that the loss of one's parents is a terrible thing and makes life such a horrible nightmare. Parents are meant to give birth, nurture and raise their children. This, however, isn't the case for an orphaned child.

With determination and the proper mind set, great things can come from the grievance. If I weren't an orphan I wouldn't care at all about the real person in me, at least not as much as I do now. My own journey has encouraged me to start up something that can make a difference and give hope to an orphan. Through the little resources around and with the help of a number of friends I have been able to start up Shalom for Africa. The birth of Shalom for Africa is to make a difference in the life of the poor of the poorest.

I have learnt to live for others and not to be selfish. Life is worth the sacrifices we make. I want to help and make those around me comfortable. If you can't see the good in the departure of your parents then make the good out of the life you have ahead of you. It all starts with you.

You and I can be the voice of the voiceless in the world. Join me, make a difference.

Chapter 6
2012 UPDATE

With the background of a volunteering for charity and the drive to attain my dream of making a difference in the life of an orphaned child, I was so convinced that my own experience could be used to give hope to the hopeless child in the world. My own experience gave birth to Shalom for Africa, a charity organization that is to give hope to orphaned children and single mothers in the world. Shalom for Africa's mission is to improve the conditions of vulnerable people, especially orphans and single mothers, by providing them with education, basic materials, and medical care, helping families start up self-sustaining projects. Life is never easy when you have no one to turn to for love, care and guidance. Shalom for Africa is aimed at giving love and hope to those who are hopeless with a dark and futureless dream.

Along this journey with the help of a network of friend's I have also taken this dream as far as Texas. Shalom for Africa is now registered in Texas, USA. We have been blessed with 45 acres of land on which the Shalom for Africa village is going to be built. On this land an orphaned child will be given the chance of education, a family, healthcare and a place for worship. On this land in Nakasongola is where an orphaned child's dream began. My hope is to build a permanent orphanage where the needy children will experience the best conditions for their personal development, as well as increasing the likelihood that they will become important contributors to their community development after completing schooling. A preschool for the baby and young orphans, a primary school, a secondary school, and a vocational school that will be used as a training ground for the big children and single mothers to attain skills in projects such as faming and agriculture, crafts and bead-making, and sewing. On this land I am hoping to have a rehabilitation centre, a children's play park, worship centers and farmland to provide enough food.

Mase is not waiting for the future but rather using his talents to create one, not only for himself but also for the hopeless and abandoned child. You and I can change the world and everything around us. So, come and change the world of an orphaned child. It does not take much to change the life of an abandoned and hopeless child. Your love and care can wash away their tears. This dream does not end with me or in Nakasongola and Texas. I see the future of changing the life of an orphan in and around the globe. Please join me make this dream a reality.

IT WON'T BE LONG BEFORE YOU TOO REALISE YOUR DREAM, KEEP CHASING.

About the Author

Paul Masembe lives in Nakasongola, Africa where he dedicates most of his time to helping orphaned children. Being an orphaned child himself he understands firsthand the challenges that are connected to being orphaned and so he has written his story to share his story. He has crossed many obstacles to be in the position he is today with the ability to write a book. He is to be commended for his strength and determination. Let's help him make his dream of building a better future for orphans a reality. By reading and sharing his you are helping to also change the world of an orphaned child. It does not take much to make a difference.

www.ingramcontent.com/pod-product-compliance
Lightning Source LLC
Chambersburg PA
CBHW031255290426
44109CB00012B/596